In Sea

A Celebration o

Miracles

Because God's Grace goes before us
to make the crooked paths straight,
it's important that we remember
to stay out of the way.

Lorraine Brown, March 1997

Billie Sue,
May you be as blest reading as I was in writing—
Lorraine
Christmas '97

MIRACLE CREATIONS

In Search of My Self,
A Celebration of Miracles

ISBN 0-9657653-0-X
LCCN 97-93392

Published by:
MIRACLE CREATIONS
P.O. BOX 871381
MESQUITE, TEXAS 75187

Printed by:
BROWN BOOKS, LTD.
A division of Personal Profiles, Inc.
DALLAS, TEXAS
(972) 381-0009

Cover and Book Design by:
LAURA D. WILSON
fit to print
DALLAS, TEXAS
(972) 248-7776

Printed in the United States of America
First Printing

Table of Contents

Section One

My Life: God's Gift To Me, My Gift To You

Section Two

My Poems: God's Gift To Me, My Gift To You

Section Three

My Wisdom: God's Gift To Me, My Gift To You

Acknowledgments

First, I want to acknowledge, with thanksgiving, my Higher Power, my Heavenly Father/Mother God, my God who lives in and through me, for entrusting these words of knowledge, encouragement, inspiration, faith, hope, love, peace, and joy to me, which enabled me to recognize and believe in miracles. He is the Author, I'm only the scribe. I know this book was given to me to heal my wounded soul. This was accomplished as I began my marvelous recovery journey as an incest survivor. This led to my awareness of my spiritual journey which is what this journey through life is all about. I gratefully, with love, share with you what I've learned.

Next, I want to acknowledge my first "Recovery Angel," Dr. Angela Kavas, Psy. D., through whom God worked to challenge, guide, teach, and encourage me. Like any wise teacher, she didn't give me all the answers. Instead, she taught me how to find them on my own.

I feel this book is a part of her because she was used to prepare the soil, to plant the seeds, and she nurtured them through germination until I could nurture them myself. She encouraged me to keep a journal which is where this book was created. She told me I had a gift for writing.

I was also blest during my first forty months of healing, to be challenged and guided by three other "Recovery Angels," Lu Vorhies, M.A., Lisa Urech, L.P.C., and DiannaLynn Rumsey, L.M.S.W. – A.C.P. God brought each one into my life, at a specific time to work on particular issues. They each had their responsibility in the development or growth of this book because of their participation in my learning to search for my Self.

I want to thank my best friend, the father of our five children, Jim, for over thirty five years of marriage and the learning experiences from that union. I appreciate the love he gives me and enabling me the opportunity to learn about real love which sometimes means letting go.

A special thanks to Karey and everyone else at Personal Profiles who were so very helpful in the delivery of this precious Miracle.

To the rest of my family, friends, group members, and co-workers, who have so graciously listened, prayed, shared, read my poems, cried with me and now celebrates with me, I thank you from the bottom of my heart; to all the other authors whose books I devoured; those who passed the torch to me and hung around to guide my writing; those writers of today who accepted my letter of thanks, especially those who took the time and energy to write or call me offering encouragement, thank you; to all the strangers who have touched my life since I've been on this planet, thank you. You have all, in your own different, yet same way, been an important part of my life that has enabled me to experience the miracles which made this book possible. To everyone whose help made it possible to get this miracle in the hands of those who are ready for it, thank you.

Dedication

I choose to dedicate this book to my loving, free spirited daughter, Terie. All through my journey she has been a wonderful supporter, friend and daughter. About seven months into my recovery journey, I was sharing with her and my oldest daughter, Gena, my collage that I was doing for a group therapy session. I had many pictures of lonely little girls and as I started talking about them I started feeling the pain of loneliness that my inner child had numbed while growing up. As I was crying, Terie said, "I wish I could just take her into my arms and hold her."

I told her that was all that little girl ever needed. Terie took me in her arms like you would a little child. As the three of us cried, Terie very softly prayed, "Thank you, God for bringing my mom through all this. I just ask you to please make something beautiful from the ugliness of all this shit."

I believe this book is only the beginning of the evidence of the answer to that simple prayer. Yes, I believe in miracles.

Foreword

Humanity
4 Where Ever U R
On Your, Life's Journey 77777

Today

Dearest Reader,

It wasn't long into my recovery journey that I started hearing, "The mistakes we make, the pain and the suffering that we go through are our teachers. They are our learning experiences."

It was almost two years and lots of pain later before I thought to ask the question, "What in the hell am I supposed to be learning?"

This book is an attempt to share with you not only of what I have learned, but the experiences, and the teachers that helped me learn.

If you are thinking that this book is about a hardened criminal, a menace to society who has made a great transformation because of a Damascus Road experience you may be disappointed. I'm just a regular person, just like you who has tried to live a good life in the sight of God and man. However, I had wake up calls, as we all do, that sent me on a miraculous search.

A long time ago I learned that if I wanted to know about something, whether it was sales, sewing, decorating, children, an illness, butterflies, mythology, philosophy, importance of fat in baking, whatever, all I had to do was look in the encyclopedia or find a book on the subject. I could learn from the experience or research of others.

I had no idea that I would be learning by writing my own books sharing my own experiences. It was then that I learned that to really know something, I had to experience it first hand. Other wise it was only borrowed information. Who was the wise person who said that experience was the best teacher? Mom West always said a bought lesson was better than a borrowed one.

In the beginning it was through the quietness and stillness of journaling, which I believe became my conversations with God, that I started receiving poems. Later, all I had to do was to get still and quiet and the insights or thoughts would go across my mind like the weather report goes across the TV screen. They never interrupted anything, they were just there. Sometimes I had pen and paper handy and could write, but sometimes I didn't. Sometimes I would get the thought again and sometimes I wouldn't.

This writing has been fascinating to me. It was through this inner searching that my Higher Self chose to reveal and continues to reveal Its Self to me. As my mind became renewed, as I learned to overcome fear and ignorance, I was able to find wisdom and love.

Though there were times that I wondered, I didn't know for sure until recently, that for the past four years I have not been writing just one book. I have actually been writing two.

This first book, *In Search of my Self, A Celebration of Miracles*, is a preface or an introduction to the second book titled, *I Have Crossed Over the Bridge*. In that book I will be sharing more extensively of the lessons that I have learned and that I am continuing to learn. I will be sharing of the miracles which happened within me to form my opinions, concepts, and perceptions. These two books together are my Spiritual autobiography which I am sharing as two letters. These are my gifts to God first and then to Humanity.

In Search of my Self, A Celebration of Miracles is a book about my journey searching for and discovering my Higher Self. I didn't know it when I started, but this was the Self that I was really looking for.

On the first page of my first journal, which I started in September of 1992, I wrote: "Getting to know me; Rosa Mae Gray, Mattie Lorraine West, Mattie Lorraine Brown."

Several months later in my second journal I wrote: "Getting to know the Real me; Rosa Mae Gray, Mattie Lorraine West, Mattie Lorraine Brown."

In the third and fourth ones I wrote: "In search of myself."

I had been Baby Rosie, Mary's daughter, Jim's wife, Gena, Terie, Mark, David, and Donna's mom. I had been Auntie Raine when I took care of children over twenty years ago, Rainy to some of my friends, and I was the Tupperware Lady when I sold Tupperware. I am Nanny to my precious grandchildren. I have worn lots of different hats in my time.

During my search, I also found that while growing up, I had worn many different masks. I became whatever anyone wanted or needed me to be. All they had to do was either be nice to me or threaten me, it didn't matter. It seems that I carried some of these masks with me even as an adult. When it came down to it, I didn't know who or what the real me was all about, so I thought it was the real human me that I was searching for.

If the self that I have been searching for was my human self, I could leave you with the following two paragraphs and there would be no need for the rest of this book. However, I found that there is much more to me than this physical form.

I am an Aquarius with a Libra moon. I've only recently learned that we Aquarius are outgoing, independent, curious, and intelligent. It has only been in the past couple of years that I have developed independence, became aware of my curiosity, and felt intelligent. I had thought that one had to have letters after their name to be deemed intelligent or to have any self worth. Because I was in sales for so many years, I developed, through the "fake it 'till you make it idea," an outward outgoing personality.

The Aquarius symbol is the "Waterbarer." This means that we came here to the planet to get Wisdom (water) and share it with others. My Saturn, where my soul sets, is in Gemini. Gemini are thinkers, speakers, writers, and communicators. I didn't know this until my manuscript was almost ready for publication. I had never had the desire to write or speak until I started and found that I couldn't stop. This makes me know that these writings are from my soul.

I was told, "*Yes, indeed, it is a wise person who reads this book. The Universe will be a better place because of it.*"

I know that I have become wiser in writing it and I believe the Universe will be a better place because I did. In essence, these books will never be finished for others will come along, after I've left the planet, pick up the torch and keep sharing knowledge as more healing takes place. I will be here in Spirit cheering them on.

In a peculiar way I have felt like a researcher unconsciously obsessed with a theory and searching for a healing substance for a dis-ease called, "Spiritual Amnesia." The intriguing thing to me is that I feel that I have, at the same time, been the subject for this experimental research. I've dissected my whole life in front of you in the following pages. I have put myself, my thoughts, my ideas, my feelings, my beliefs, my opinions, my perceptions, and my concepts under the microscope of humanity because of my love for the Universe.

Because of my soul wounds, it has taken a Miracle of healing grace to overcome the fears that would have hindered me in presenting the results of my research to you. There have been times when I would hit a brick wall, (which I had erected), when things didn't come out the way that I thought they should, and doors didn't open as I expected. There were times when doubts and fears kicked in and I wanted to give up and throw in the towel. I wanted to quit. I wanted to run. There have been times when I begged God to take me on and then me come back at another time with a healthier self, more knowledge, more understanding, more courage, more money, more support, more time, more, more, more. He so patiently and lovingly would say, "*If I did that you wouldn't need me and then you would forget me even more. You wouldn't learn about trusting me to help you remember and that is the whole purpose for you're being here. Don't you remember that you are here to help teach others to remember. It's when they see your perseverance, your getting up when you fall, your keeping on in spite of fear and doubts, that will help kindle that little spark. You volunteered to do this. Are you changing your mind?*"

Have you ever been driving at night and someone flashes their head lights off and on to signal to you that you had forgotten to turn your lights on? How did you feel? My response is usually to first feel stupid for not remembering and then to feel gratitude because that person was used by the Universe probably to not only save my life, but others as well.

When you have been on the other end and you were the one giving the signal, how did you feel? Did you say to yourself, "there's a stupid so and so who forgot to turn on their lights? Guess I had better signal them before they get us all killed."

I think not. There was probably the feeling that said, "I've been there and done that and felt grateful that someone signaled to me before I ended up killing myself and maybe others."

Or maybe you didn't need to stop to think or feel anything. It was just a natural response to signal. It was like an instinct. It was just a random act of kindness, love and compassion.

The writing of this book is kind of like my flashing my lights to those who are not using their lights because they not only forgot to turn them on, but may have forgotten they even have any. The purpose for writing this book is to share the knowledge of the faith and courage that I have found. I do this with the belief that it will ignite with a spark of the faith and courage of those who need it so that they can learn to become the creative expression of their Higher Self which I feel is the reason we are here on this planet at this moment.

It seems I am always being asked, "What is your book about?" I've found that this is not an easy question to answer. I have explored for four years now and I'm still searching for the correct response. Some will say it is just another self help book; some will feel encouraged or inspired by it; some will think it is completely off the wall; some might be afraid of it because they will think it a bit mystical. Whatever your perceptions or your gut reactions, I invite you to open your mind and heart so that you are able to think for yourself and draw your own conclusions. Try to side step some of the already false limited information that has been programmed into you consciousness and listen to your soul. Listen to your little voice within.

Sometimes, when we read or hear something that may be a little different from our old beliefs, or the information that we have been taught all of our lives, our ego or the human part of us sends out feelings of fear. I can assure you that what ever questions, doubts, disagreements and most any other feelings you feel as you read this book, I have experienced the same while writing it. Emily Cady, in her book, *Lessons in Truth*, stated that when new information is mixing with the old, chemicalization takes place, not only in our mind, but in the cells of our body. This may even cause some physical discomfort. I liken this to when an antibiotic is introduced to an infection. For about twenty four hours there is a battle going on inside and we may find we feel a little worse. What you are going to read may create a little confusion and that is a good thing. That means you are thinking and are open and receptive to learning. However, at this point some of you may choose to set this book aside for a while. That's perfectly all right. You will pick it up again when you are ready. If what you read resonates with your spirit, rejoice and thank your Creator. If it doesn't resonate at this time, just bless it and then release it back to the Creator. I believe there is a divine order for our lives. I believe our soul knows when it is ready to receive or experience certain things. Some of you, because it is the right time on your spiritual journey, may begin to ask questions. By honoring your soul's need to "Get Knowledge" you will find yourself being led on the most remarkable miraculous journey that you have ever or will ever experience. You will have begun your own search for Truth.

You will find in the back of this book a mini workbook or journal if you want to jot down some of your own thoughts, feelings, or questions. This will make this book more personally yours.

I was sharing my analogy about the car lights with some friends and one mentioned that in certain parts of town gang members would drive without their lights on and the person who flashed their lights was their next victim for a random shooting. Immediately, in my humanness, I felt fear. However, in the same instant I was reminded that I have nothing to fear because I am protected at all times. At the same time I know that I'm not attached to this life or its outcome. If per chance I was shot and killed, then that was the way I was to make my transition and leave the planet. If I was shot and wounded then I would have other challenges to learn from. I will not allow fear to keep me from doing what I feel is the kind, compassionate, and loving to do. I will not allow fear to hinder me from my doing Good.

When I was writing certain parts of this book and the next one that's to follow, the information was a little different than my perceptions of some of the old beliefs that I was taught growing up. Some of the new things that I was writing I found it hard for even me to agree with, or should I say that my ego didn't want to agree with, yet I knew in my soul these thoughts, these words came from the Spirit within. Then I felt some fear concerning what friends and relatives that knew me might think or feel about me after reading what I wrote. I knew this was just another lesson in trusting the Spirit within. I did not want fear to keep me from doing what was kind, compassionate, loving and Good so I asked God, "Are you sure You want me to write this? What are people going to think?"

Just as clear as a bell His answer came back, ever so gently, "*That's the whole idea, I want my children to think. Far too long they have been satisfied with the scraps that have been thrown their way. Because of fear, ignorance, and lack of motivation to search for themselves, they have been satisfied with the "second hand knowledge" and "hand me down faith". Far too long they have lived through the "borrowed" experiences of others. They have been the victims of Spiritual Amnesia and Spiritual abuse long enough. I want them to know they don't have to be limited or satisfied with this narrow minded existence any longer. It's time they wake up and become aware of the choice to take responsibility for finding their own soul's healing of their Spiritual Amnesia, so that they might remember their own Truth. It's time they remembered their Higher Self. It's time they remembered who they are, where they came from, why they are here, and where they are going.*"

So, this book is an epistle written to you, sharing A Celebration of Miracles. Miracles that I'm finding on this journey, In Search of my Self. I have tried to write, not to tell you what you should or shouldn't do, or what is right or wrong, but just to share my own experiences as I searched for the knowledge that led me to the awareness of my Higher Self.

The words in this book or any other book will not change your life, but the Spirit who is woven through each page will guide you to search within for a Higher understanding. We are so blest to read and hear from other people as they share their beliefs, concepts, understanding, and perceptions, which they have found on their journey and we do learn from them. However, it's not by what is manifested through their words, but it's the Spirit who guides us into finding the knowledge that we need to bring about changes. Sometimes the Spirit plants a seed and because it takes time to germinate; it might take days, weeks, months, years, or maybe life times before we see the fruit. Sometimes the Spirit is like oil that is added to the fire within our souls and we know a change of thought takes place immediately. We only truly learn as we search and by allowing the teaching or the wisdom to come to us from the Holy Spirit. It is then that we discover from within ourselves, the Truth. I trust this book will challenge you to courageously seek your own Truth. That experience in itself is life changing.

This book was conceived in love and through the illusion of immeasurable pain. It grew from what seemed at times as unbearable pain mixed with more than equal amounts of unspeakable joy. It is now delivered to you with much love from a peaceful contented soul.

I wish I could truthfully tell you that I am the author of this book. It has never been a life long dream of mine to write. I never consciously ask for this privilege, but I guess inviting God to live His life through me opened my creative doors. I am but a scribe chosen to record certain events of my life's journey. I wrote as I received from the Author/Creator of our lives. This was something I had to do. I couldn't not write, even if I had wanted to. The words spilled out through my journals and my poems. They would come to me at four in the morning, while on my morning walk, throughout the day while driving, taking a shower, while listening to someone else talk, or before I went to bed at midnight. They would come in the midst of grief and the midst of joy. They became a passion, an obsession. They became a

Healer.

You may find, as I did, that the Truth I share is not totally unfamiliar. It may be packaged a little differently, but there is one thread, LOVE, that seems to run through it as did the writings of King David, Solomon, Bro. Paul, Ralph W. Emerson, Charles Fillmore, Emilie Cady, Kahlil Gibran, Helen Steiner Rice, Dr. Peale and all the others who, after remembering who they were, spent their lives delivering this message. When they made their transition, this Truth, this torch, was passed on to evolve in the lives of those who came later. If one believes in such things, because the same Spirit dwells in each of our souls, maybe they are right here with me, even now, guiding as I write. I'm wondering if it might be possible that they are at the key boards of the more contemporary writers like, Peck, Kaye, Schuman/Thetford, Williamson, Hays, Moore, Chopra, Northrup, Dyer, and Redfield. If we are all one with God, with the Universe, are we not all one on this eternal journey? In Hebrews 12:1 the writer writes, "*that because we are compassed about with so great a cloud of witnesses,* (who do you think these are if not the souls that have gone on before?) *let us lay aside every weight; (old baggage, every mistaken thought, false belief, fear, and ignorance); anything that could so easily hinder us from running, with patience, the race that is set before us*" (or fulfilling our purpose).

If we look, with our human eyes, at the lives of some of those earlier writers, we see what looks to be lives lived in poverty and loneliness. That is but another illusion. When we look through our spiritual eye we can see that they were more prosperous than some of us will ever be, because they were true, honorable, loyal, courageous, and trustworthy not in a human way, but spiritually, to that which they were called. They knew their purpose. As far as being alone, how can one be alone when one is guided by all these souls gone on before. There is a vast difference between feeling alone and choosing solitude. The difference being choice.

Speaking of choices; as you continue to follow me on my journey, you can choose to see and hear me as a person diagnosed or labeled as having Borderline, Histrionic, and Dependent personality disorders. (I'm wondering who is questioning and will take the time to aquaint yourselves with information on these disorders. If you learn nothing else from this book, please listen to that part of you that questions. That comes from your soul.) Personally, I think I might have even had a little of some of the other personality disorders, as well, as does most of us here on the planet.

These disorders were the effects of early childhood losses coupled with a childhood filled with physical, sexual, verbal, and emotional abuse with a little emotional neglect thrown in. The prognosis, or prediction of likely outcome, is usually (in the human mind) quite poor for these personality disorders because these maladaptive patterns of behavior have often taken a lifetime (forty eight years for mine) to develop. Changing them, even being aware of the changes that need to be made, is in itself a miracle. I was given prozac and told that I would probably be taking it for the rest of my life.

In my search I found that if I wanted to choose to give my power to or make these disorders my "higher power" and remain a victim of the effects and a slave to ignorance and fear, I could certainly do that. It was perfectly all right if I chose to continue to experience that hell. Farther along in my search, however, as I received knowledge, I found I had other choices.

It is my hope that as you follow my story you will see and hear me as a person, maybe not unlike yourself in some ways. I hope you will see me as a person who continues to enjoy the wholeness as I receive the healing from these disorders and have not taken prozac since November 1995.

I hope you will see me as a person who, because of the miracles of Grace, has gained insight and knowledge; who with the caring of the soul, now experiences joy, peace, and love from within; A person that, because of emotional pain, was motivated to embark on a life changing journey; A person who has found and crossed the bridge from the, "life's a bitch and then you die," attitude to the, "Life is an adventure of Celebrating Miracles," attitude; A person who has found a purpose to live, who has no choice, but to share these personal experiences for the hope, faith, inspiration, and encouragement to others. I hope you choose to see me as a person who can truthfully say, "I am thankful for my dysfunctional, abusive, emotionally neglectful lost childhood."

For a semblance of clarification I want to familiarize you with a few terms that you will find sprinkled through out as you read. So there will be no misunderstanding about Who my God is, I will refer, mostly with the masculine pronoun. God has no gender. He, just like the angels, is androgynous. He is my Father when I need one. In Isaiah 66:13, God says she will comfort me as a mother comforting her baby. She is my nurturing Mother Goddess when I need one. In Psalms 23, He tells me He is my Good Shepherd ever watching over me, guiding me and keeping me safe. In Psalms 91, He speaks of being One with sheltering wings, like a big eagle or maybe like an angel.

To get our attention we may experience a "cosmic monkey wrench" thrown into our wheel of life, a "cosmic two by four" up side the head, or a "wake up call." They may come to us in the form of dis-ease or any thing that causes us the feeling of being out of control or a dissatisfaction with life. Sometimes they come in the form of questions and a desire to search. What ever form, it is a reminder from our soul that it is being neglected or abused. This is Grace.

For those not familiar with the term "God Deal," my interpretation is; God's Grace in action, a blessing, a gift, or just the right timing. When looking at something and knowing that God brought that event, that book, that person at just the right time. It's one of those things that happens in divine order and you know it is ordained of God. You may have heard it referred to in the past as a coincidence, synchronicity or a serendipity.

Thank you for choosing to permit me to share with you the miracles which I'm experiencing on my journey.

Section I

My Life: God's Gift To Me, My Gift To You

"Man struggles to find life outside himself, unaware that the life he is seeking is within him."

Kahlil Gibran's *Secrets of the Heart*

In The Beginning ....

Some people believe that before we were even a thought, before we were conceived, before we came to this planet, we chose our parents. We chose them depending on what we needed to learn during this lifetime to enable us, as the Spiritual Beings that we are, on our spiritual journey back to where we came from, to grow in knowledge into the perfection that we already are. I'm told we choose our experiences, our challenges, our circumstances, our mistakes, our mates, our professions, everything just so we can grow as we remember who we really are in God.

As I've lived, learned, and wrote for the past four years of the first fifty three years of my life, I have to admit that this journey has taken some unusual twists and turns. I have learned that everyone in my life is a gift and is here to bless me and to be blest by me being in their lives. Sometimes when someone is cutting in front of me in traffic or seems to be rude for no apparent reason, I have to remind myself that they are in my life to bless me. Every time a cosmic monkey wrench is thrown into my life, I have to ask, "how can I look at this circumstance in a way to be blest? How can I be a blessing to that person? How can I grow spiritually from this experience?"

It was about two years into my recovery, after working with several wise therapists before I had grown enough to learn to ask these questions. God, gently reminding me by keeping those questions at the front of my mind, helped me to survive the hell (useless unnecessary suffering and pain) that I endured while searching for my answers. From a human point of view my life makes no sense, but whose does? Looking at it from the spiritual understanding or through God's eyes, it makes perfect sense. If we do indeed choose our life, this is the life I chose. I thank God for every lesson I've learned and for all the ones I'm still learning.

After many conversations with God, I've decided to share some of the appalling details of this drama which I have been living, not to make you feel sad for me, but for you to see the beautiful fragrant miracles God has so lovingly brought forth out of the manure covered childhood I survived. I know why I chose this life and I hope you will too, after you complete this part of my journey with me. I don't have all the details, but it all started something like this:

On February 13, 1944, at 8:00 in the morning, a little baby girl named Rosa Mae Gray made her noisy entrance into what is known as life. I'm sure all her screaming was because she somehow knew what was ahead in her new adventure and she would have preferred to return to the warm safe place she had just left.

The first person she met was her Mommy, Gracie. Of course she had known her for the past nine months, but now she got to see what she was like on the outside. She saw her Daddy and saw how he smiled at her Mommy.

When they arrived home from the hospital, her big brother Earvin, who was seven, was there. Neither one was too sure about the other.

Later, her nineteen year old half sister, Rosie Lee came

by. Rosie was expecting a new baby any time so she didn't stay long.

Then came another half sister, twenty one year old Birtha Mae. She had a little boy about six. Somehow Birtha Mae had known that the new baby was going to be a girl so Mommy Gray allowed Birtha Mae to choose the name, Rosa Mae which was lovingly taken from both sisters' names.

Even after all this, I think if Baby Rosa had her choice, she would still like to have gone back.

During the next eight months after being held, sung to, played with and loved by all these people she decided this wasn't such a bad place after all. In fact she felt just as loved, safe, and warm as she had felt inside her Mommy.

One day Mommy Gray had to go back to the hospital. When she came home this time she didn't have a new baby. Instead she had found out that she had uterine cancer. The knowledge of cancer was limited back then so Mommy Gray knew that she didn't have long before she would have to leave the planet.

Can you imagine how painful it must be to have a new baby and know that you would never get to see her grow up? I guess you could choose to be a slave to the pain and grief, be bitter, dwell on all that you would be missing out on, and probably hasten your leaving; or you could find the courage to accept what was happening, be thankful for the time that you had, make the most of every day, every hour and every minute. I believe that Mommy Gray talked to God a lot about taking care of Rosa Mae as she grew up. I believe that even after Mommy Gray left the planet, her spirit was always with Rosa Mae. I believe at this moment wherever she is and what ever her mission, she knows what is going on and is celebrating.

Because of hospital stays, and not being able to care for Baby Rosa when she was home, Baby Rosa stayed with one sister and then the other and sometimes Birtha's sister-in-law, too. They were all busy with their own families, but they tried to make a place for this little baby. Baby Rosa Mae wanted to go back to her Mommy where she felt warm, safe, and loved. She didn't like being separated from her Mommy because it was like being separated from one's self. How can one be separated from one's self and survive?

Just fourteen months and one week after giving Baby Rosa this gift of life, her loving gentle Mommy had to leave her prematurely. She had to leave before getting to teach Baby Rosa what she needed to know to live this life she had given her. She had to leave before seeing the baby take her first step, before seeing her off for her first day of school, talking to her before her first date, before she had the chance to meet her grandchildren. She had to leave before Baby Rosa was old enough to tell her precious Mommy how much she loved her. As with all babies her Mommy was her God, her love. They were a part of each other. One day she was there, the next she was gone. She seemed to just disappear.

Judith Virost, in her book, *Necessary Losses*, wrote that the pain experienced by a child under the age of six losing its Mommy is likened to the pain of being doused with oil and set afire. For Baby Rosa Mae this kind of pain, which created a great wound in her soul, could only be coped with by numbing and forgetting. Otherwise death was a surety.

Because Daddy Gray was a fisherman and felt that he couldn't give this baby girl what she needed, he, with unselfish love, allowed an older childless couple to adopt her. So, within about four months, the rest of her family, along with the identity of Rosa Mae Gray, was taken away as her Dad, brother, sisters, nieces and nephews disappeared and her name was changed. Baby Rosa Mae had to disappear just like everyone else in her life.

Though she went to live with Clint, age sixty five and Mary West, age forty five, when she was about a year and a half, Mattie Lorraine West wasn't officially born through adoption until about four months later. She had a new family.

Mom West had survived breast cancer, the Depression, having a husband in the war, and had followed him from one logging camp to another until they bought a little country store with the living quarters attached, in the middle of nowhere in Arkansas. She had become one strong tough lady. She was a wonderful cook and took pride in her flower gardens. She made Baby Rosa's clothes and was a help mate to Daddy West. She adored "Mr. West" as she called him. Daddy West felt his life was complete now that he had a beautiful baby girl. Though she wasn't walking when she went to their house to live, it wasn't long before she started running to keep up with her new Daddy. She was the apple of his eye. He played with her and loved her, trying to replace the joy, love, and trust that had been yanked away. Rosa Mae quickly became a "Daddy's Girl."

Four months later, a month before the adoption was final, after beginning to adjust to a new Mom and Dad, new house, new rules and a new life as someone else's daughter with a new name, it started happening again. Daddy West disappeared.

Mom West proceeded with the adoption. Because of all the love and attention I had received from Daddy West, it hadn't mattered much that Mom West wasn't gentle, affectionate, warm, and soft. I had not noticed the huge walls of protection she was building around her. She couldn't give the love, attention, and nurturing this baby, still recovering from the grief of the early losses, needed so badly. We both grieved in our own way, alone. We both stuffed the pain; Mom by working hard and me, a two year old, again by numbing and forgetting, creating more wounds in the soul. Neither knew how to help the other. I feel part of Mom disappeared along with Daddy.

Mom ran the country store pretty much by herself while maintaining a nine acre farm with pigs, chickens, and a cow named Bossy. Mom shared Dad's love for animals so there were lots of dogs around the store. Our home place was a good place for people to drop off unwanted dogs and cats.

At the age of three or four, my life's journey took me down a different road when Mom married a man named, Hamp. I remember the wedding was on a Friday night and took place at our home.

I know it was a marriage of convenience so Mom would have some help. I remember that he didn't sleep with Mom and when I woke up Saturday or Sunday morning he was in my bed sexually abusing me. At the same time I remember a rooster crowing. (It's neat how God gives back just a little bit of memory at a time. About two years into my recovery, while I was eating an ice cream cone, I remembered Hamp saying to lick it like an ice cream cone.)

I don't know if Mom found out or not. I know he was only there for the weekend before disappearing. I have sketchy memories that make me believe that Mom might have shot him as he was chasing me down the driveway. I don't remember the two of us ever talking about him while I was growing up.

I had a great time living in the country. I loved to play in the white sand close to the store. I could take three or four Coke bottles filled with water and play for hours building roads and tunnels. I have happy memories of playing in the clover trying to find one with four leaves. Some how I knew I needed some "good luck." I would make necklaces from the clover flowers and pretend I was somebody special. I would lay rocks and sticks to mark room boundaries of my "house" under the sheltering limbs of a tree that had little flowers on it. I played at being a cowgirl, straddling the fence behind the house. I had a great imagination.

I played alone most of the time except when some of the customers brought their kids. Most were African-American and Mom didn't like my playing with them. I never understood why because in my eyes, the loving eyes of a child, I couldn't see where they were any different than us.

Our pasture backed up to the St. Frances River and there was a draw bridge that I found fascinating to watch. I would hear the ship's horn and would run through the pasture, dodging cow patties, just as fast as my skinny little legs would carry me so that I could watch the bridge bend in the middle and the huge ships go under. I would stand under the pecan trees and wonder where those ships were going, and who was in them.

I remember sometimes on Fridays before dark, Mom would close the store and we would work together at a job she had on the side. I would chase the chickens into a corner of the chicken yard so Mom could catch them. She would ring their necks until their heads came off and while the body flopped around the yard, I would throw a wash tub over them until they stopped flopping. I remember being spellbound with the way the chickens could still do that without their heads.

Later, after we had killed about ten chickens, Mom would heat boiling water and using the same wash tub, dip the chickens into the boiling water to make picking the feathers a little easier. She would stay up sometimes past midnight cleaning the chickens. She would get up early the next morning and before opening the store, drive to Marianna, about ten miles away, to deliver the chickens to a supermarket. I wonder how much she was paid.

There were a few people who came into my life while living in the country who were safe and I have wonderful memories of them. I'm so thankful to have had them in my life to fall back on, reminding me that everyone didn't hurt me.

Brother McDonald stands out. For one thing I think he was the tallest man on earth. He was the pastor at the little country Baptist church about four miles away at Brickeys. He always came by to pick me up on Sunday mornings, Sunday nights and Wednesday nights to take me to church. He was soft spoken and smiled a lot. He was safe and I love him for being there.

An older couple named Applewhite lived a few miles away. I loved going to their old farm house, because it was so big. Mrs. Applewhite let me churn the milk and help gather the eggs. She also played paper dolls with me. We would use the Sears and Robuck catalog for the paper dolls as well as the clothes. Sometimes I would even draw, color, and cut out my own clothes. What I really loved was an old musty smelling room with the piano. She let me play all I wanted. When I was about seven or eight I could pick out, with one finger, "What a Friend We Have in Jesus," "Amazing Grace," and "Just As I Am." I don't remember what it sounded like, but they said it was beautiful.

Another couple who were good friends with my Mom were the Owens. They had a furniture store in Marianna. We went there about once or twice a month. I loved playing house on the furniture. Mr. Owens always had Juicy Fruit gum for me.

I thought he was the coolest person ever because he could push his teeth out. It was a mystery to me for I tried as hard as I could to learn to do it, but I never could get mine to come out.

In the summer when I was about eight years old, my cousin Jack's two sons, ages fourteen and sixteen visited and while we were left alone they both raped me. They explained the blood on the sheets and the pain I was in by saying I was playing on the headboard of the iron bed and hurt myself. For whatever reason, I didn't say any different. Again, the memories and feelings were pushed down and caused more wounds to my soul.

Occasionally, when Mom wanted to go to church we would attend the Baptist church in Marianna. That next Sunday morning Mom and I attended the church there, and I made my "profession of faith" by asking Jesus into my heart. At that time I made the decision out of fear because I didn't want to go to hell. I was told He would always be with me and would never leave me. I certainly needed someone to take care of and love me. God honored that child like faith.

That evening we went back for the evening service and I was baptized. I remember it was summer because I wore a sun dress, with the jacket, of course. It had a flared full skirt with the buildings of New York City on it. I remember they had to put weights on the bottom of the skirt to keep it down.

Later, when Brother McDonald found out, he didn't understand why I joined there instead of his little church. I remember feeling bad because I had hurt his feelings. I know now that by thinking of his feelings, I didn't have to deal with mine. Again I could numb out and kind of forget.

I'm wondering if this is when I started carrying the guilt and shame for what was done to me as well as feeling bad for hurting the feelings of others. I wanted so bad for everyone to love me and not be mad at me. In my sub-conscious, I had developed a fear of rejection and more abandonment.

Also, during that summer, I had to go stay a week with Daddy West's brother and his family about forty miles away in Hughes. They had two daughters, ages ten and twelve. They had a room full of dolls. Their mother made lots of doll clothes so we played for hours dressing the dolls. This was the first time I had ever stayed away from Mom West. That night when I went to bed I experienced, what I know now, to be separation anxiety. It was much more than just home sickness. I was hysterical screaming and crying for my Mom. They didn't yell at me or tell me to stop. They were patient, gentle, and understanding. They held and comforted me for hours. Unlike before, I had someone to grieve with. They let me choose all the dolls I wanted to sleep with and I finally calmed down and drifted off to sleep surrounded by about ten or twelve dolls.

In the spring after my tenth birthday we were literally scared off our property. I remember as if it was yesterday, hearing the shots being fired at the store that night. Mom said she couldn't get any help from the sheriff because he was in on it, too. I remember the fear and thinking how brave Mom was. As she fired back I remember being so afraid that she would kill someone and be arrested or she might would be killed. I didn't know what would happen to me, or where I would go.

They finally left and a few days later we were packing to move. She had to sell our home and livelihood for practically nothing and we moved to West Helena.

We rented a little house on Anderson street, a couple of houses away from my Mom's sister, Aunt Ora and her husband Uncle Henry. Their son, Jack, who had kids older than I, and two of their divorced daughters were in and out all the time.

You would think with the new family close by, maybe some of my emotional needs would be met. NOT. For the next six years, along with the indoor plumbing and neighbors who lived within a few yards instead of a few miles, the piano lessons, the church going, being a Girl Scout, getting my first bike and my first pair of skates, also came more sexual abuse from twelve or so different people, that I remember. There was also verbal and physical abuse as well as emotional neglect and abuse. This continued until I married at age sixteen. By this time I was getting really good at the numbing out part, but some of the memories wouldn't leave. Maybe because so much was happening.

I remember growing up trying to be the perfect daughter. Because Daddy Gray had given me away, I lived in the fear that Mom would send me away if I was bad. When the sexual abuse was going on, I couldn't let Mom know because then she would know what a bad girl I had been. I stuffed the guilt and shame, along with the other pain. Eventually, I became so comfortable with my false self, that my true self disappeared behind the false mask. I became what ever anyone wanted me to be. I had no identity. Mom was forever being told what a good job she was doing raising me because I was such a good little girl.

My cousin Jack, who was the father of the two boys who raped me when I was eight, was also a perpetrator. Once I started retrieving my feelings and memories, bleach, body odor, and the smell of stale cigarettes triggered a lot of the memories of my encounters with him.

In the fall when I was ten, I was raped on the way to school. You'll read more details about that later in another section.

I think I was an angel once when I was about eleven. I went with Mom to Mr. Gregory's farm where she picked strawberries, peaches, and cotton during the season. While she worked I found many ways of amusing myself, because of my keen imagination. I took books to read and I would day dream a lot.

On this particular day it was quite warm even early in the morning. I found some protection from the heat of the sun under the shade of a huge tree. I don't remember exactly how it happened or why I thought of it, but as I was borrowing this shady refuge, I became interested in the house that shared the same yard with the tree.

I had checked at the house earlier to see if there were any kids that I could play with, but no one was home. The house wasn't much to look at, a shack really. Weathered wood, a step missing, just the over all appearance showed not much care or expense went into its upkeep.

Before I knew it I was inside the house surveying what needed to be done. Some how little skinny me managed to pull all four of the bare urine scented mattresses, out into the sun to air out.

I gathered up the dirty clothes that were scattered around and washed them by hand with water that I brought in from the pump outside. Because it was so hot I didn't make a fire in the wood stove to heat the water. I just washed them in cold water. I hung them on the clothes line out back. I knew with the sun beating down they would be dry in no time.

I swept and mopped the splintered wood floors with the rinse water from where I had rinsed the clothes. The floors didn't shine, but they were clean and smelled better. I washed the dishes and cleaned the kitchen.

Later I dragged the mattress back in. They were dry and warm from the sun. I think they may have smelled a little better.

I brought in the clothes folded them and left them on one of the beds.

There were some roses growing wild in the field next to the house so I picked some. I found an old brown snuff jar and filled it with water. I placed the roses in it and left them on the wooden table in the center of the room.

It was about that time that my stomach reminded me that I had forgotten to eat my sausage sandwich that I had brought for lunch. I sat my weary body under that same huge tree thinking about the day. It had been so much fun pretending that this was my house, but at the same time I had been running on pure adrenaline from the fear that the rightful owners would return and find me there.

I tried to imagine the reaction of the people coming home tired from working in the fields all day and finding their surprise. Part of me was afraid they would be angry that someone took such liberties of invading their house and privacy. Most of all I felt warm and fuzzy inside because no one would know what I did. I just hoped the people would be happy.

I never told Mom because I was afraid she would be mad that I went into some stranger's house. I don't remember ever telling anyone until now. I often wondered who lived there and what their reaction was. Thinking about it after all these years still brings that warm fuzzy feeling inside. I know now that feeling is called joy. I'm still amazed that I could drag those mattresses out. There must have been other angels there helping, too.

When I was about twelve we moved to Cleburne Street. Aunt Ora and Uncle Henry had also moved and lived three houses from us. The school that I went to was only a couple of blocks away so most of the time I would walk to Aunt Ora's house for lunch. She always had my fried egg sandwich ready. After school, I would stay there, tho I would probably have been safer at my own house. Uncle Henry, who was Jack's dad was also a perpetrator during this time. I still have dreams sometimes about ordeals with him. His younger son, Harold who was about six years older than I, as well as the first two cousins were telling me by this time that they would tell Mom if I didn't "do it." If it wasn't so painful this could almost be a slap stick comedy. You would think with all this activity they would bump into each other or something. I remember thinking I must have a sign somewhere on me that read a little stronger than, "kick me."

Mom had to work on Saturdays at a department store. She would come home on Saturday night, after nine, after being on her feet all day, and take me to the skating ring so I could skate for an hour or so. She would stand there and watch. This was our togetherness. I know this was one of the ways she showed her love for me. Wonder if she ever thought about letting me bring a friend. Now that I think of it, I didn't have friends because anyone that I would try to be friends with, Mom called trash. Loneliness is the feeling that I have when I think of my childhood.

One Spring evening when I was thirteen, my next door neighbor, who had molested me on another occasion, raped me. His two brothers were there, but because most of the memory is still blocked out, I can't say for sure that they raped me, too. I remember it happening in the front seat of an old car in his back yard and I remember his two brothers holding my legs. I woke up in my bed several hours later and I still don't know how I got there.

It was about nine when I woke up. I knew Mom would be home in a half hour or so and I still had to go to the store to get the coal oil. Because of that fear, I was able to pull my self together and block out all the events that had transpired that evening thus creating more wounds to the soul.

I'm not sure when Mom told me that I was adopted, but sometime after the rape, I remember being angry at Mom for something. I knew I had a Daddy somewhere so I wrote him a letter. Of course I told him how bad Mom was and would he please come and get me. I had no idea where to send it or if I even intended to send it. Mom found the letter. She screamed and yelled saying that if I wasn't happy there she could send me to a much worse place. She was talking about the girls detention center. She said that my Daddy couldn't take care of me even if he wanted me. I decided I had better straighten up my act and be grateful for what I had.

It was also during this time that an old man a few blocks down the street molested me. He never touched me below the waist because he said that was only for my husband.

When I was about thirteen or fourteen Mom had a friend with a son named Tommy. Tommy was thirty five and was mentally handicapped. He was gentle, sweet, innocent, and safe. He loved unconditionally. He looked forward to my coming to visit with him because he always wanted me to play the piano for him. I enjoyed this time together because I loved seeing him smile and he never hurt me. He was a safe person to be with.

Also, when I was about fourteen Mom took in a twenty eight year old roomer named Ralph and his little boy, Leon. Leon was about three years old and I loved helping to care for him. Ralph had been married to Leon's mother whose name, oddly enough, was Rose when she was fourteen.

Ralph wasn't there very long before seducing me with his warmth, charm, and attention. We enjoyed singing while he played the guitar and sometimes I would play the piano with him. I visited his room several times a week and enjoyed the secret fantasy role of wife and mother. When he left to move to Little Rock he rented me a post office box and wrote to me some. He even sent me a set of rings showing his intentions. Before long he stopped writing and we lost touch.

A year or so later I was playing the piano at a little Baptist church. My best friend, Alice had a brother named James who was about four years older than I. We three rode to church functions together. James and I doubled dated with another couple. He was always a perfect gentleman, and never tried anything inappropriate with me. In my warped thinking, I thought there must be something wrong with me. Why isn't he treating me like everyone else? At the same time I was afraid he might find out what a terrible person I was so when his cousin, Jim came home from college and started paying attention to me, I dropped James.

I met Jim in the summer when I was fifteen. I found out from his sister that his birthday was September 24. We were attending a Bible study at a different Baptist church. I went in that night all dressed up in an orange and yellow flowered dress and black patent leather shoes. I walked up to him as he was talking to his friend Josephine and wished him a Happy Birthday. He thanked me and said I was the only person who had wished him Happy Birthday. Josephine said she had not known that it was his birthday and he said, "Somehow, Lorraine found out."

That was on a Thursday night and on Sunday night he asked if he could take me home after church. I tried not to sound excited when I broke the news to James that Jim would be taking me home. In my heart I was already fantasizing about being his wife and him taking care of me.

When school started a few weeks earlier, Mom had given me money to pay for my school fees. Because I'm such a procrastinator, I had just stuck the money in my purse and forgot about it. One Sunday afternoon, following a nap, I walked into the front room where Mom was standing holding my purse and the money she had given me. She was so angry. She was screaming that I was a whore. I tried to explain about the money, but she kept calling me names and picked up my shoe (the black patent leather) and started hitting me with it. A neighbor from across the street came in and pulled her off me, telling her to calm down before she had a heart attack. I went to my room to cry alone. I went to church that night with bruises all over. I wore a sleeveless dress so they could be seen. However, I didn't get much attention.

I went with Jim to his family's Thanksgiving dinner. His brother Gene and wife, Dean had just had a new baby girl a few weeks before. A couple of weeks after the Holiday, the baby died. Everyone who had been exposed to the baby had to take some medicine to ward off any possible infection, so Jim brought some of the pills to me. The next day after school, Mom, without saying a word about it, took me to a doctor to be examined to see if I was pregnant. She thought Jim was giving me pills because I was pregnant. Of course the doctor informed her that though I wasn't pregnant, I had been sexually active. I felt so ashamed, so violated, so alone, and so unloved. Again I had to stuff those feelings in order to go on living. (I have to stop here and give thanks for the miracle of Grace that with all my sexual activity, I didn't become pregnant or receive any sexual disease.)

In January Jim joined the Air Force. At lunch time, just before he left town, he came to my school and picked me up to go to lunch. I promised to write every day, and for the eight months that he was away, I did.

Just before Christmas, Mom had started taking care of a lady who had suffered a stroke. I remember when Mr. Lewis brought his wife to live with us. I was a little afraid of her at first. Pretty soon we warmed up to each other. She couldn't be understood very well when she talked, which was very frustrating to her because her mind was still good. Because she was bed ridden, I would hurry home after school so I could brighten her day. Sometimes I would help her sit up in a chair. She loved for me to read to her, especially the Bible. I would play the piano and sing for her. I would brush her hair. I loved her because I could be her caretaker. She was as good for me as I was for her. Because Mom had so many other responsibilities, she was short on patience with Mrs. Lewis. Sometimes Mrs. Lewis would soil her bed and Mom would yell at her. Mrs. Lewis would try to yell back in her crying voice. Sometimes Mom would hit her. When I saw this happening I was confused because I didn't know what I was supposed to do. Part of me wanted to tell Mr. Lewis on one of his monthly visits. I wanted to yell at Mom to stop. But I couldn't do anything because I was afraid it would make her mad and she would send me away. I would just cry with Mrs. Lewis later and we would try to make each other feel better. I tried to do more of her care so Mom wouldn't be so tired.

Mrs. Lewis started to get worse. I think she was giving up. Because of her having to stay in the bed so much, she developed horrible ugly bed sores. (As I think of my soul wounds that I received from my childhood, I liken them to those repulsive pus filled oozing bed sores.) I don't know if Mom was neglecting her and not turning her or what, but she was really bad. The stench in her room was nauseating. I tried to clean it every afternoon with the pine oil hoping to rid it of the offensive odor.

In April when I was sixteen, I came running in from school to find Mrs. Lewis not in her room. The bed was stripped, and the windows were wide open. I thought maybe her husband had come to take her for an outing. I found a note from Mom saying I had gotten a letter from Jim. She said she was at the funeral home and for me to come there to get it. I was so excited about the letter that I jumped on my bike and took off.

When I arrived at the funeral home it was dark inside

and Mom was whispering so I tried to keep my excitement quiet as she handed me the letter.

I'm not sure when I became aware that Mrs. Lewis was gone. I don't remember if I read the letter before or afterward. Everything after that is still blocked except in my mind I can still see this little girl sitting in a chair close to the casket. She's crying softly thinking if she had told Mr. Lewis about the abuse, maybe his wife would still be alive. This was all her fault.

Four months later Jim came home from the Air Force on leave and one week later, at the tender age of sixteen my dreams came true and we were married.

Eleven months later our first daughter was born. Through the next fourteen years, two more daughters and two sons later, there were a few affairs, which I later found out was a carry over from the earlier abuse. I was still looking for that love and attention I didn't have. I had no boundaries and didn't know I could say no. Because I had long since learned to be whatever others expected me to be, I wasn't aware of personal rights or choices.

Yes, I did remember bits and pieces of the sexual abuse. However, I didn't know about the effects of the guilt and shame I was carrying. I stayed numb because if I allowed myself to feel the pain then I would also have to feel and believe that I was worthless and undeserving of love. I would be undeserving of life. I would feel dirty and unlovable. As it was, I could see no reason for anyone to love me. I knew if they found out about the secrets, if they really knew what a bad person I was, they would hate me and I would die and surely go to hell. This made me try harder to be the perfect wife and mother. I couldn't afford to make mistakes or I might would be sent away or left again.

Since I had no role models of what a "happy" marriage was, I had my own fantasy made up from what I read in True Story magazines and what I saw on television watching all the family shows. I waited on my knight in shinning armor hand and foot. I tried to anticipate his every need, I was always a willing sex partner. It was like I had to make myself worthy of his love and attention. I had to make up for his marrying such a bad person.

Starting in 1967 we spent about five or six years in a "Total Life" Christian ministry, kind of like being missionaries. There were schools, nursery through Bible School, radio program, printing, and lots of other enterprises to help support this mission outreach center. If you wanted to give your life serving God they had a place for you. Here I found a family. I found love and acceptance.

It was also here that I really understood what I had done as that child of eight. It was then that God honored that child like faith and I came to know Him as my life. I learned that He lived in me and I in Him. It was then that I appreciated this marvelous gift He so freely gave to me. It was then that I had a revelation of God as my Heavenly Father. A Father who accepted me as I was. A Father who would never leave me. A Father who would always be there with me to guide and teach me. I surrendered my life to Him, not from fear, but because of what He had done for me. I worked hard to be perfect so He wouldn't be disappointed in choosing me as His child. I worked hard to try and be worthy of my salvation.

The Word was taught by gifted people and my relationship with my Heavenly Father grew. I know it was a place that God dwelled. I believed I had found a place to find redemption through works. I found happiness. Being the mother of three kids I graduated from the high school as Salutatorian. I went to Bible school and taught Kindergarten. We had our meals there and we only went home to take baths, do laundry and sleep. When we weren't working or going to school we attended worship services. I thank God for that place. It was a beautiful experience in my life.

Though most everyone tried to live "in the Spirit," we were still human with the "freewill" to make choices. Mistakes were made and the place was closed. This, again was a big loss for me and I had to adjust to living in "the real world." I went church shopping, but tired of it because I felt I wasn't being fed. Maybe it was because I didn't give them enough time so I could find a place to "work." Maybe God wanted to have this time to bring me to a place so He could teach me in His own way. I missed the fellowship of sharing and hearing about the faith building experiences from other people.

Some years later, I found another family through my Tupperware business. Being a successful manager for sixteen years, I received recognition, gifts, took trips, enjoyed a company car, and made good money. I was good at demonstrating the products and servicing my customers. I was a helpful caring manager to my consultants. This helped to build my self confidence and I became more independent, however, I was still hiding behind my mask. I guess my caretaker role actually helped me in my business. After about a year into recovery, I was unable to service my customers properly so I chose to retire. From this family, I still enjoy many friendships.

During these thirty two years of marriage, I believed my knight would never need to even look at anyone else or talk to anyone else. He had everything he would ever need at home. It seems my knight in shinning armor, who I thought was going to take care of me forever, be the daddy I never had and live only to make me happy while I only lived to make him happy, didn't know about this fantasy of mine. He was great taking care of the physical things we needed, but just like my Mom, he didn't know about my emotional needs. Besides my own emotional baggage I brought into the marriage, he had brought along his own baggage. Bless his heart, one minute I was acting like his Mom taking care of his every need, and the next I was the little ten year old still looking for that daddy to give safe love and attention. You can imagine the confused mixed signals that we were both sending out and receiving.

After the children had left home to make their own nests, I guess it was time to work on me. Though I had received "wake up calls" in the past, it wasn't time for me to wake up, but this time I had a "wake up call" that awakened me. It was the general life's questions and confusion and the childlike needs that brought me to therapy at age forty eight. I went with the sole intention of finding out what I needed to do to get Jim to make me happy. After all, I had spent all these years catering to his needs so I figured the wise therapist would hear my story, call Jim in, and tell him what he needed to do and say to take care of my needs and then I would be happy. You can imagine my bewilderment when on that first visit she said, "you can't depend on or expect him to change or to make you happy. You are the one that will need to change. You are responsible for your own happiness."

She recommended two books, *The Dance of Anger* and *Co-dependent No More*. This sent me to the library to get a library card which I hadn't had in years. I got through the books by half heartedly reading them.

When I went back for my second visit, we talked about the books and then she asked a question that would change my life. "Do you remember ever having been sexually abused as a child?" (As I write this, I have heard that there is a group trying to get a law passed where by a therapist could no longer ask this question as it might plant a suggestion and promote False Memory Syndrome. It will be up to the client to take the responsibility, find the courage, and share this information with the therapist. I encourage and support you to find the courage to do this so you can experience your soul healing.)

Of course I did. I started telling about Uncle Henry, Jack, the next door neighbor, and the old man down the street, just for starters. I was talking about it as if it was a movie I had seen, until I looked in her eyes and saw such pain. She very quietly and gently said, "I am so sorry that you were abused by those people. How do you feel about this happening to you."

I sat there for a long time because, for the first time I didn't know how I was supposed to answer. I had never really thought about it, much less felt it. I couldn't remember anyone ever asking how I felt about something, before. The few times when I was sick were the only times I was ever questioned about how I felt. Somehow I knew this wasn't a physical feeling she was asking about. How was I supposed to feel? How would anyone else feel that this had happened to? What was I supposed to say. How was I supposed to be acting? For forty eight years I had learned to say, act, do, and be what I thought everyone expected of me. I realized I couldn't feel my feelings. This became the first step of this remarkable Recovery Journey, In Search of My Self.

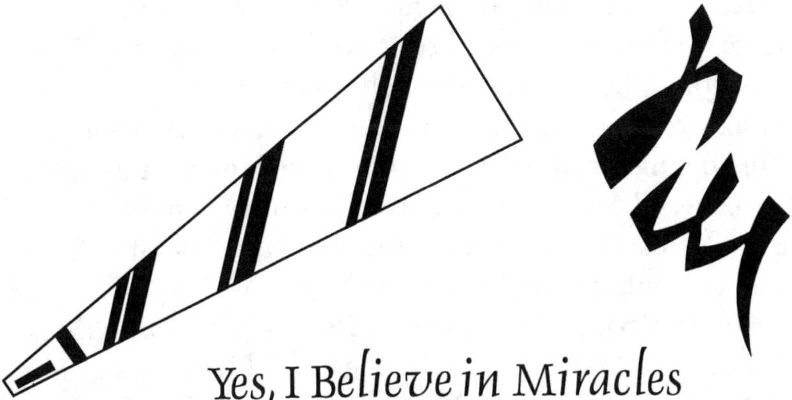

Yes, I Believe in Miracles

"And could you keep your heart in wonder at the daily miracles of your life, your pain would not seem less wondrous than your joy."

Kahlil Gibran's *The Prophet*

I shudder as I remember my friend's words ringing in my ears over and over again, "Suicide is just not an option. Life is so precious. I don't understand how you can even think about it."

I couldn't understand it either. I had no doubt that I was a child of God and He was with me on this journey. Through the past nineteen months of healing from abandonment and rejection issues, which were an effect of the premature losses I experienced as a baby and the trauma of my neglectful abusive incestuous lost childhood, God had been so marvelous. Though there were times I really felt angry with Him, and I let Him know it, He was forever boosting my faith with "God Deals" or blessings along the way. It may have been the right book jumping out at me from the book shelf at the precise time I needed it. It may have been a comforting word from a friend just when I seem to be at my lowest. Then there were the times it was the small quiet voice inside that I learned to listen to. He would wake me up early in the morning to give me fragments of inspiration for a book about this wonderful Recovery Journey I had started. So many times after a painful time I had to relive, He blest me with a poem. Yes, I knew He was with me on this journey.

So at this particular moment, I really felt confused because I didn't understand these feelings and I certainly didn't know what to do with them. A few weeks earlier, I had experienced more painful memories. I was experiencing feelings of grief for my early childhood losses. These were a lot of losses for an adult to handle, but for a baby, it was impossible. My coping skills of numbing and forgetting, which I used for the next forty eight years, had been working quite well. When I entered therapy, I learned that I had a lot of changes to make. I had a lot of unlearning and relearning to do.

Now it seemed the feelings of rejection, abandonment, helplessness, and hopelessness, were forever being triggered by events of the day. At night, if I slept, I had horrible nightmares. I couldn't seem to get away from my painful lonely past. I didn't see things getting any better. Even if I made it through the pain this time, I knew it would be back to visit again. Because I was in a twelve step program for incest survivors, daily I was doing the steps, admitting to God that I was powerless over the abuse and the effects, turning it all over to Him, but I still had no peace. I felt so tired of it all. I was tired of trying to fight to survive. I cried a lot not even knowing what I was crying for. I would go through intersections hoping someone would run a red light and take me out of all this misery. My prayers were not to help me get through this, but to let me die. I didn't want to live in this pain.

At the library I found a book, *The Courage to Grieve*. I

cried most of the way through it, but I learned that I was going through the natural order of the grief process. It had become the right time for me, as the adult, to grieve and mourn all those early losses that I couldn't do as that infant. The depression was a normal part of that process.

Though I found out what it was, it didn't make the pain any less and I continued planning on how I was going to take my life. I'm probably the only person with a "to do" list of things to do before I died. I was even going to buy my adult children copies of *The Courage to Grieve*. I find it just like my Heavenly Father, that while I was doing all this planning, I was still taking care of myself, getting my annual physical, watching my diet, going on with the every day routines.

I attended an incest conference and one of the survivors, who was dying of AIDS, kept talking about purpose. It really annoyed me. I thought they were all fools wanting to live with all this pain. Why not just end it all and be done with it?

The next morning I was awakened early needing to write in my journal about this subject of purpose. For the rest of the week I wrote and thought of little else, but purpose. A few nights later I had a dream. I awakened with the clear interpretation. The whole concept being that as I was feeling comfortable with the cold arms of death closing around me, God sent someone for me to rescue. First, the someone was me. Then I saw others, like yourself that could benefit from my experiences. I had to choose to leave that false security. God so lovingly had shown me my purpose to live. From that dream God gave me a beautiful poem titled, "Death's Arms," reminding me of where He had brought me and what my purpose was. This book is but one vehicle to carry out my purpose for being on this planet.

I'm wondering if some of you may be reading this and asking what credentials I have for writing a book, what education do I have, what degree do I have, what letters do I have following my name? I'll have to be honest with you. My education has mostly come from the school of "HARD KNOCKS." Actually, God Is My Source (GIMS) in everything for my life. I have the faith to believe that everything that I will ever need is within me.

While it's true that I'm not a well known celebrity or a Doctor, I have read a lot, I have listened a lot, I have experienced a lot, and I talk with God a lot. I've always heard that experience is the best teacher. Some of the wonderful doctors and other writers have not experienced the losses, the abuse, the pain, and the healing that I have. They have had to rely on the experiences of their clients and others. Their books have been so helpful, encouraging, and answered many questions during my search for knowledge. I feel very privileged and thankful that now I can share with you first hand information.

Section Two, *My Poems: God's Gift To Me, My Gift To You*, is my story, in poems, of how I learned to acknowledge, grieve, accept, and rejoice. These poems are indeed a gift. It was through them that the Holy Spirit taught me. You'll be aware of some repetition. That's because the Holy Spirit, being a wise teacher, knows that repetition is one of the best ways to teach. Besides, I have found that if I didn't learn a lesson the first time, it came back around so I got to practice again and sometimes again.

Through these poems I'm still gaining hope, inspiration, encouragement, and faith as I learn to internalize the knowledge I receive from them. As I would write one, I would be so overwhelmed with the reality of God's grace, that I would set here and cry tears of joy. Sometimes now when I go back and read one, I still feel that joy. I still cry. I feel such awe at the way God works in our lives.

In Section Three, *My Wisdom: God's Gift To Me, My Gift To You*, I'm sharing some of what I've learned and what I'm still learning. Because I am still learning, the information in these pages will not be complete and will be carried over into our next book. Therefore, the information in these pages are strictly my experiences, my opinions, my perceptions, my views, my beliefs, my thoughts, my feelings, and my theories. If they make you think, disagree, or agree that's good. If you get inspired or even angry enough to do some searching for yourself, that's even better.

For someone who grew up not knowing about rights, choices, and not allowed to have opinions, or to feel, writing this book is truly a miracle.

The reason I'm publishing this is to let you know I am a person just like you. Because I'm a Spiritual Being having human experiences, as a wife or ex-wife, mother, and grandmother, friend, co-worker, etc. I still make mistakes. There are so many things I would like to do differently if I could go back. The only thing we can do about those experiences is to accept them, learn from them, and then let them go.

I experience joy, and pain just like you. I have regrets just like you. I experience fear and disappointments. There have been times I've wanted to die and there have been times I couldn't get enough of life. I'm a unique creation of God and have been blest beyond measure and want to share with you. I don't have a monopoly on God's love, wisdom or grace. I don't have a monopoly on God's miracles or His gifts. We don't have to pay for them with "good works." Sometimes we don't even have to ask for them. They are provided for our delight, for our enjoyment as well as to boost our faith. God gives them because He delights and receives pleasure in our Joy.

This book is for those of you from dysfunctional families, those who have a "lost childhood." Maybe you haven't known about the need to mourn that loss. Maybe you aren't aware of the soul wounds that have been created. Maybe that's why you are not feeling "happy." Maybe that's why you choose to be a workaholic, lack self confidence, are codependent, are sick physically all the time, or abuse drugs or alcohol. Maybe that's why you seem to find yourself moving from one unhealthy relationship to another. I'm wondering if you have ever given any thought to what you might really be looking for. What need do you have that isn't being met and have you ever thought you might be looking in the wrong direction... Please listen to your soul's yearnings.

This book is for those of you in recovery programs, or you who are thinking you need to be in one. I'm wondering have you thought about what you are really recovering. Do you feel that you are recovering from something or are you trying to recover something that was lost or maybe something that you never had? What are you really searching for? Maybe you feel you need help, but you don't know what you need or where to get it. Maybe you need answers, but you don't know the questions to ask. You just know that life stinks.

This book is for those of you who are not too sure about this God stuff. All of our lives we have seemingly had hell fire and brimstone shoved down our throats until we have wanted to throw up. After all, how could a God of love allow this stuff to happen? Why didn't He stop the abuse? Why didn't He protect? Why does He allow children to starve to death. Why does He allow tornadoes, earthquakes, and hurricanes to destroy lives? Why does He allow the Jim Jones and David Kereshs or the bombing in Oklahoma? Why does life seem to be made up of one catastrophe after another? Why? While I share some in this book, I will share more extensively of my thoughts and feelings concerning these questions in our next book, *I've Crossed Over the Bridge.*

This book is for you who are aware of the spiritual journey that you are on and sometimes you are concerned whether or not you are "doing life right." I consider myself an expert on this subject.

This book is also for you who think you came from a normal family with a normal happy childhood. You had the perfect Walton or Cleaver family. You knew you were loved and accepted. Someone was there to protect you. Your folks didn't drink too much. They spent time going to your ball games and piano recitals. Maybe they taught you about God by living a Godly life in front of you. Reading my story, hopefully, will make you feel even more thankful for your good fortune as you enjoy that miracle. If your folks are still alive and you haven't done it in a while, I encourage you to go right now and call them or write them a note and thank them for what they gave you. Thank them for making mistakes and not being perfect. Can you imagine how much harder it would be to try to walk in their perfect footsteps?

Yes, I believe in miracles because I have experienced miracles. When I see a sunrise or a sunset, when I see the beautiful colors; the blues, mauves, silver grays, reds, oranges, yellows and gold amongst the beautiful puffy clouds; when I see a big round moon at six thirty in the morning in the west and the big round sun at the same time in the east; when I see the sun shining brightly while it's pouring down rain; when I see the seasons change; when it's dark and cloudy and I'm reminded that behind the clouds the sun is shining; when I smell the sweetness of honeysuckle, or caress a pink rose smelling it's perfume; when I drive through Dallas and see the skyline and think of the knowledge and work that went into constructing those tall buildings, I believe.

My precious grandchildren have taught me a lot about innocence, life, and miracles. When I hold my newest gift of love, baby Kaitlin who looks so much like her Mommy; when I rock baby Sarah, whose life is a double gift, and watch her sleep; when I watch toddler Jake love and kiss his new baby sister, Kaitlin; when Jessica runs up to me saying, "I love you, Nanny," and teaches me about holding hands with the angels; when I take my oldest grandchildren, Donald, Justin, and April out for pizza or to the park and am able to become like a child laughing, swinging, and sliding with them, when I see how healthy and how loved they are, I see God's Grace in action, and I believe. ...with childlike faith... ....become as a little child....

When I listen to my adult children and the wisdom they have found; when I feel so much love from and for them; when I watch them as a Mom or Dad with their children; I'm so thankful for the miracle that God performed in making up the lack for what I didn't receive growing up. He took the eight months of love and attention I received from my birth Mother and multiplied it just like He did with the loaves and fishes. Though I made a lot of mistakes, I know that my children have no doubts about my love for them. They are blest with loving responsible partners to share their journey through life. Our family has been blest with great health, no premature losses or fatal accidents. I know we're experiencing miracles.

When I think of the partner, the wonderful father to (me) and my children, that I was blest with for thirty five years, I see more miracles. Through the three years of recovery, he was the most patient person I've known. However, we both have had to make some changes. Because of our growing and after being honest with ourselves and each other we chose to lovingly let each other go and are divorced. We love each other and are still a big part of one another's lives. We are the very best of friends.

When I visit with a friend, sometimes listening and giving hope, sometimes sharing my pain and receiving hope, sometimes sending and receiving cards, sometimes just having a good time bowling, seeing a movie together or splitting nachos, then I know how blest we are to have this gift called friendship.

When I experience serendipitous. When I find a good book that was put on the shelf just for me at just the right time, when I turn on this computer, thanks to my son David's patient teaching to get me started, when God took over and helped me to understand the tutorials, when I "accidentally" learned about "book mark," "page break" and various other things just at the time I needed to know them, when I feel such thankfulness for the writers long ago who wrote with quill and ink by the light of a candle, and then when I'm able to experience the modern technology of today, I see how God keeps up with the times, and I believe in miracles.

When I look at my life today, when I see how far I've come, when I see how much I've changed. When, with fear, I find the courage to take risks. When I feel so much love from within that I feel I'm going to burst if I don't share it with someone. When I learn something new and know it is really mine because I've internalized it which means it made it from my brain to my heart. I know then that it is really mine and no one can take it from me. When I read the poems in this book, yes, I believe in miracles.

I never had in mind to write or publish a book especially one with poems. To be honest, I never really cared for poetry, maybe because I didn't understand what the poets were saying. That may be because poems come from within where there are feelings, and my feelings were numb. I had never written a poem until Thanksgiving Day, 1992. I almost didn't include it in this book because it wasn't "deep" like the others. Then God reminded me that it was a gift from Him just like the others. He reminded me that I had experienced the simple miracle of smell. At that time in my journey, I was just learning about feelings and I was experiencing the feeling of joy for some things that I had taken for granted before. You will see the difference in my growth when you read my poem for the following Thanksgiving, 1993.

I remember in school having assignments to write poetry, but like a lot of other parts of my childhood, the creative part was numb. However, since I've been on this journey and have thawed out, it seems the creative part of me has come alive. God has been blessing me so prolificly with the poems and as I've been sharing them with friends and family they have encouraged me to have them published. I know these poems are a beautiful gift from God and that I am to share them with you.

I've talked to a couple of friends who shared for the first time of their story of their past. One in particular comes to mind because she admitted that she might have some stuff that needs to be worked on, but she really doesn't want to do it. Why dig up the past? Why go through that pain? She was doing okay with it. Yet it bothered her enough to bring it up. She spoke of several things that she was experiencing that I could relate, from my own experiences, to the debilitating effects of her sexual abuse.

I look back at where I was almost five years ago before beginning this journey, and where I am today. I look back at that part of me and feel sad because I know there are others out there, just like I was, in so much pain, but not knowing the reason. Now I see, feel, and know the difference. I can testify to the reasons to dig it up. It's called HEALING. It's called EXPERIENCING THE GRACE OF GOD. While it's true that we can't change the past, I found that by bringing the secrets to the surface; by looking at them; by feeling the pain; by grieving; by accepting; by giving the whole ugly mess to God to make something beautiful from the manure; by forgiving myself, as well as others, I could allow God to heal the soul wounds which kept me in the bondage of ignorance and fear. I have found that the ignorance and fear is what hindered me from really knowing God and from experiencing the love, joy, and peace that is mine.

Because I dated the poems, you can see where I was at different times of my journey. Maybe you can find when I went from the victim, to the survivor, to the thriver to the overcomer.

I know when on a recovery journey, everyone's journey, though it be the same, is taken differently. People do their life's journey, as well as their recovery journey, differently because people are different. There is no right or wrong way to do them. There is no time frame. I can laugh now because I've heard others say the same thing, but I remember when I started therapy, almost five years ago, that I thought I would go a few times and I would be "fixed." Even when Dr. K. told me it would take a commitment on my part and it would be painful, I thought, "I can handle anything for a few months. It can't be any worse than the pain I'm experiencing right now." (By the way, I have to be honest and tell you that the pain was worse, but well worth it.) I feel that it is a miracle that I am where I am and I arrived here so quickly.

God first blest me with a wise therapist, Dr. Kavas, who did not hand me a bottle of pills and tell me they would alter the chemicals in my brain so that I would look at life differently.

Another thing she did was not give me all the answers. Instead, she challenged, guided, encouraged, and suggested ways for me to find them for myself. Doing it this way, I learned to search for answers and to depend on the God within, thus I was able to experience the miracles and you are able to be reading this book.

One of the wisest suggestions she had was for me to start keeping a journal. I will be eternally grateful for that because this book was born from those writings. I will never forget how I felt when she told me I had a gift for writing.

She always saw the strength in me though I couldn't see it myself. She reminded me constantly what a strong courageous person I was. She provided a safe place and with her I was able to let surface the painful past with the memories and feelings. I was able to learn about the self defeating effects of the soul wounds that I was living with so I could learn to change the things that were harmful for me.

Because she was a safe person, I developed a love and trust like I had with no other person. Because of this, and with her wisdom, I was able to develop a strong foundation so I could then learn some of what I wasn't privileged to learn while growing up. In a way she became that loving nurturing mother that I didn't get to grow up with. She nurtured the part of me that needed it which enabled me to begin to learn about love and acceptance for myself. I learned that I was worthy of love.

I believe God performed a miracle in that He allowed me, through Dr. K., to experience the feelings for Mom Gray that had never been allowed to be expressed. He allowed me to give and receive the love we had both been denied. I have no memories of my birth Mother, but because of the miracle of the Mother transference with Dr. K. I am now reminded and think of my Mother when I think of Dr. K. It is such a blessing to have something that brings her to mind. Yes, I believe in miracles.

In a way, I feel that God used Dr. K to save my life. Certainly because of our work together, I was able to find this new life I enjoy today. I love her for being a willing vessel and allowing God to work through her as she became my "Recovery Angel." I love her as much as I could love anyone who saved my life. Working with Dr. K., He allowed the grief of the separation anxiety to surface. He allowed me to feel the grief that I, as the little baby had felt, but didn't get to acknowledge before.

Because of the "crisis only" part of my insurance, I was limited to the number of visits so our client/therapist relationship had to end prematurely. As we came closer to time of termination in October of 1993, it brought up the issues of separation anxiety and feelings of abandonment and rejection because of so many of the people I loved had disappeared from my life. All of a sudden I was having to not only live through the pain of our separation, but also the feelings that were triggered of the past. I tried to get more visits, but the answer was no. I decided I wasn't going to take this lying down. For the first time ever I was going to fight for what I needed, which was more visits to feel closure with this separation. I wrote letters pleading for my life. The answer was still the same. Again more feelings of rejection and abandonment. It was more than I could handle and because of the feelings of hopelessness and helplessness, I decided to take my life. Because my youngest daughter's first baby was due anytime, I chose to wait, not wanting to take away her joy. My younger son was getting married at the end of November and then December and Christmas would follow.

I didn't want to die, yet the pain was so overwhelming I didn't want to live. I finally wrote Dr. K. telling her of what was going on. It was decided that because I was suicidal, I was in crises and was allowed twelve visits in 1994 to get closure on our termination.

On April 14, 1994 we said good-bye as client/therapist. It was a beautiful experience. I miss her, and feel sad because I can't continue to share with her the miracles I'm experiencing, but I'm so thankful for the experience of our working together and the knowledge that she will know when she reads this book. I'm so thankful that God allowed our lives to touch and yes, I believe in miracles.

I believe that this was my first lesson in learning that living is learning to let go and moving on to the next chapter or evolution of my life. It's when we try to hold on to old stuff; beliefs, people, relationships, and other things that we create more bondage and we can't experience true freedom. We choose to hold on to the old because of ignorance (we don't know any better) and fear (because we are afraid to take the risk of experiencing the unknown.)

For about six months before terminating with Dr. K., I was also attending a therapy group for incest survivors. Lisa Urech was the therapist for the first eight weeks, which was called Phase One. This was kind of an introduction to familiarize us to a group situation, which is quite different than individual therapy. When I moved from Phase One and into Phase Two, I was introduced to Lu Vorhies who was the new therapist. Within about a month Lu left and as luck (or a God Deal) would have it Lisa took over. Yes, I believe in miracles.

As time was getting closer to terminating with Dr. K., I contacted Lu and she agreed to see me as my individual therapist after my termination with Dr. K.. It made leaving Dr. K a little easier having a therapist with whom I had previously worked.

I feel blest to have been able to work with Lu. She worked with Dr. K. to force me to let go of Dr. K. by cutting off all communication with her. Then she started me on the road to learn to deal with it. She helped me to grieve. Not just for Dr. K. but for all the other losses in my life that were triggered because of the separation. Yes, I believe in miracles.

Lu taught me by challenging, but also providing a safe place to practice as I learned. It was kind of like on the job training. I got to practice with her in a safe place as I received knowledge. I've learned I have the right to disagree. Lu provided a lot of practice in agreeing to disagree. I learned that I have the right to stand up for what I believe. I have the right to ask for what I want and need. I learned about being courageous enough to take risks. I learned about dealing with not always getting what I wanted or asked for.

In December of 1993 I had remembered, with "body memories and feelings" as well as the other feelings, of being raped on the way to school in the fall when I was ten. I remembered the boy went to my school, had red hair, was about fifteen or sixteen and wore a blue, black, and white plaid flannel shirt. I could feel the pain in my wrist as he pulled me to the ditch. I could see the dried grass on the sides of the ditch and it sticking in my hair. I could see me afterwards sitting there shaking and pulling it out of my hair. I could feel me shaking from the nerves as well as the cold because my skirt was pulled up around my waist. I could remember as his heavy body laid on mine and with his rhythm, I was saying over and over again, "we're gonna be late, we're gonna be late, we're gonna be late." Guess that was the way I blocked out the physical pain. I became more concerned with the trouble I was going to be in when I got to school and that night with Mom when she found out I was late.

Being tardy or absent from school was not tolerated. I wonder if somewhere in the back of my mind I might have welcomed the punishment. Maybe I felt it would be a cleansing or a washing away of the filth that I believed I was covered in because of the unspeakable act that (I did) was done to me.

For weeks afterward, because I kept the secret, I would wake up screaming from the nightmares of being raped and then giving birth to babies with red hair. (Thinking about this, I find it amusing that Lu has red hair.) Because of that trauma, I had a terrible fear of being late. I always left for any appointment so I would arrive at least thirty minutes early. If I was running late because of traffic or weather, I would panic. It was horrible.

Lu was great to help me with this fear of being late. One day I got to my appointment with her about two minutes late because of traffic and weather conditions. I was a basket case all the way there. When I walked into her office, I lost it. It took her about fifteen minutes to calm me. She kept telling me she was not my Mom and she was not going to hurt me. Today, I still have my clocks set seven minutes fast, but I don't panic if my time is running close. Now I choose to be punctual because I don't want to miss anything. Yes, I believe in miracles.

After about seven months of our working together, I terminated my counseling sessions with Lu because I felt it was time to move on to the next chapter in my life. I felt she had contributed her part to my recovery. I felt no separation anxiety with our terminating.

All this time I had continued with my group therapy, which was a great training ground where I could learn about taking risks to say what I felt, being confronted, and practice as I learned the importance of communicating in relationships. I could even handle people being angry with me and I could disagree with someone with out the fear of them hating me.

Almost a year later, about the same time I had stopped seeing Lu, I felt I no longer needed group therapy, so I terminated that, also. Our final night together was so precious. There was only one other lady present with Lisa and me. She and I started sharing the "God Deals" we had experienced on our journeys. Lisa joined in by sharing with us the changes she had seen us make. The hour and a half session became a two hour session. At the end we all felt it appropriate to close with prayer. We held hands and took turns praying. God's presence was indeed there. Yes, I believe in miracles.

Lisa also terminated being the group therapist shortly thereafter to begin doing individual therapy. A month or so after terminating with Lu, because there were still some issues of grief with the infant part of me that I felt Lisa could better help me with, I started working with her.

She not only allowed me to grieve, but she helped my inner children grieve. She seemed to understand when I bought a sympathy card for Baby Rosie. One night I was buying get well, birthday, and inspirational cards for friends and family and somehow I made it home with one that I had picked out, changed my mind and thought I had put back. As I read it, the message seemed different than what I had read in the store. I knew immediately this was a card from Mommy Gray to me the adult. I felt that Lisa shared the same wonderment as I. Lisa helped me learn to be comfortable with feeling different. It seemed every time I went through such an experience, the healing oil of God's love was applied to those horrible wounds and healing was able to take place. She was so encouraging to me as I took control of my recovery work. Yes, I believe in miracles.

I feel that God sent her to me to be my spiritual guide. There were times I would go to see her and ask, "Lisa, what's happening to me. I don't understand all this joy, all this knowledge I'm receiving from God. I feel that something Holy is growing inside of me. I can't believe all these feelings. I don't know what I'm supposed to do next."

At the same time I sometimes thought I was losing my

mind, (which in a way I was because my mind was being renewed by God Himself through my writings.) She would say something like, "It sounds like you are wanting to be a vessel willing to be used by God. Sounds like He is using you. Just listen to Him. You'll know what to do."

With her I felt really comfortable sharing the miracles that were happening. I guess I needed her to reassure me that I wasn't going crazy. She listened and accepted what I shared. I felt she took me seriously. She was so insightful. God used her to share more wisdom about this journey. She suggested that I might want to find a prayer group or fellowship and become a part of it. For some reason that wasn't the right time, but it did happen a year or so later.

Our work together was finished after about three months and I didn't have any abandonment or rejection feelings. Yes, I believe in miracles.

Two months after terminating with Lisa, I felt I was ready or needed to work on adult issues. I tried calling Lisa, but being the wise therapist that she is, she didn't return my calls. After the third time, I knew it was time to move on. Lisa had spoken often of her supervisor, DiannaLynn and how she thought I would benefit from working with her. So I called her and told her I was ready to work on the big girl stuff.

I was blest to work with this feisty red head for about six months. I feel that I've matured twenty years at least. She helped me with the part of me that I believe none of the others were supposed to. Just like the others coming into my life when they did, I believe God sent her to help me learn to take the risk to grow up. God did some dynamite blasting through her when I was stuck. It was awesome (although I didn't think so at the time) to watch God work with us and through us. She did not allow me to be the helpless wounded child/victim in her office. She encouraged me to listen to my intuition and take the risk to live like an adult. It was later that I learned the importance of taking control of my life. How could I consciously give God control of my will and my life to work through me if I had given the control to someone else already? (As a victim we give our power or the control of our lives to whomever or whatever we feel that has made us the victim.) Only we have the ability to choose to take our power or our remote control back.

She challenged my inner beliefs and knowledge that I had received from God, teaching me that I had the Master Therapist living within me and really didn't need her. Yes, I believe in miracles.

I feel such gratitude that God has given me therapists that allowed Him to work through them. They have all been miraculous gifts from my Heavenly Father. I trust and hope they were blest by working with me, too. I feel when two people play a duet in the sonata of life that both are allowed to grow and learn.

I was privileged to be a part of an incest survivors group, which is a Twelve Step Group founded on the same principles as A A. For about the first two years of my recovery, this group was an important part of my journey. I love them and the knowledge they have shared from their own faith, strength, hope and experiences. I could call these women night or day if I was in a crisis or if I just wanted to share a "God Deal" that I had been blest with. They became a fellowship where I could share the good things God was doing. It seems at the same time we outgrew the need for the group and we stopped meeting. However, some of us keep in touch. Yes, I believe in miracles.

I grew up believing that making mistakes was one of the worst things I could do because then I saw my imperfections. Growing up I tried to be perfect so my Mom would love me and not send me away. I learned real well to wear a mask that allowed me to do and say what was expected of me. It was really hard to believe that anyone could love the real me without the mask. I didn't know who this person was, but she must have been unlovable or her Mom would have been more loving and all those people would not have left or hurt her. Surviving this was a miracle.

I have learned that painful circumstances come up for all of us throughout our life, while we are on this planet. We will always have problems that have to be dealt with. The pain we experience and the mistakes we make are teachers if we allow them to be and eventually, if we have the same experience enough times, we will learn and move on. It's when we can rejoice, be in awe at God's plan, honor Him where we are, reverence Him and His power, adore Him for the God He is, in the midst of the pain and mistakes, that we are ready to receive knowledge. It's then that the awareness of our spirituality grows. It's then we remember who we are, where we came from and where we are going. It's then when we find love, peace and joy from within.

The gifts and the miracles we receive from God are not teachers. They are there to remind us, to give us hope, encouragement, and to build our faith. They are there as part of our spiritual growth, but they are not teachers.

They are also given because God delights in giving us good things. These are pure clean gifts. He does not give them expecting anything from us out of obligation. If we give something back to Him it should be a pure clean gift not expecting anything from Him or thinking we are repaying Him. It's easy to praise God for the gifts and miracles, but it's harder in the middle of pain. There is a scripture that says, "In all things, give thanks."

Because of being loved, safe and secure, some people learn early, while growing up, how to become strong and handle the challenges that come along. For some of us things were so painful growing up that our little child learned to cope in a different unhealthy way. Because that scared little child handled things by numbing, and forgetting, that's how the adult handles things. Some adults grow up abusing drugs, alcohol, having eating disorders, denying, living in abusive relationships, and becoming workaholics to continue the numbing and forgetting. It's when we become aware that these things are not working, that we are able to begin this journey. It's then we learn the difference between merely existing, being stuck in the past, doing every thing for the future, or peacefully LIVING where we are in this moment. Since living is a daily experience, it only makes sense to do it one day at a time.

I feel, most of the time, that I am at a place where I can accept the challenges because I have the knowledge that God and I, together, can work through anything that comes our way. As I learn to concur, to acknowledge, to embrace, and to accept what I've been through, who I am, what I am, and where I am, I am able to see miracle after miracle. I have such joy, peace, and love like I've never experienced before. It's kind of like heaven on earth, because I've learned acceptance and that everything is for my good and for my spiritual growth. I don't feel at war with my feelings, my thoughts, the shouldas, couldas, and wouldas. I'm not at war with my past or my future. I'm no longer at war with myself.

I don't want to mislead you into thinking that fear, doubt and disbelief don't raise their ugly heads once in a while. I don't want to mislead you into thinking that there haven't been times during these years of sharing with you that the grief was so bad that I wanted to die. You'll read about them in the poems. What I want you to see and celebrate with me is the fact that I didn't take my life. I may have fallen, but I didn't stay down. I didn't give up. I fought for my life. I asked for help from my friends, my therapists, and my Heavenly Father. I made it through the pain once more. I received God's protection once more. I'm so thankful I'm here to finish this book. Yes, I believe in miracles.

This book is a gift of love from God to teach me on this journey. I now share this gift of love with you. This book is now for your encouragement. It's written to give you hope because I know how it feels to feel hopeless. It's written to help you recognize your Power from within because I know how it feels to feel powerless. It's written to give you strength because I know how it feels to feel like a weak victim. It's written to help you to know that you are not alone because I know how it feels to feel alone. It's written so that you can learn to accept and learn to love yourself because I know how it feels to feel unloved. Most of all it's written to nourish your faith as you grow and you learn to allow your Higher Power to teach you. As you accept His grace and allow your spiritual awareness to grow, you will find that you are becoming more aware of the everyday miracles that are already taking place in your life.

While reading, I hope that you will allow yourself not only to think, but to feel, also. This is my first four and a half years of my healing journey in poetry as well as some of the lessons I have learned through the experiences. In this book you'll read of my pain as I am learning about how my feelings of today trigger those feelings of my past. You will see how I had to learn to process them both at the same time. Most of all I want you to experience the miracles of growth and healing that takes place right before your eyes.

My hope is that this book will encourage, and inspire you to want to grow, to seek your own answers, and provide you with that little push you may need to look at your life a little closer. I challenge you to take an inventory and see if anything is lacking, and what could be changed so you can live instead of just existing. I have found such a difference in the quality of my life and it didn't have a thing to do with externals. It had to do with me on the inside. Again, if after looking at your life and everything is just the way you want it and you wouldn't change a thing, please take a few minutes and thank God for miracles and somehow find a way to share your gifts with others.

I honestly, with thanksgiving. believe that it is no accident that you are reading this book. I ask that before you continue, that you ask your Higher Power, as you understand Him/

Her to give you what you need from these pages for your spiritual growth and awareness on your journey through this life. Do I really believe that God can do that? Yes, because I believe in miracles.

The invariable mark of wisdom is to see
the miraculous in the common.
Ralph Waldo Emerson

We're One Day Closer

As we pulled off the little dirt road into his driveway, I thought that my heart was going to come leaping out of my chest at any moment. It had been forty hours since I had spoken with his wife and made the plans to visit. All the way to his house, and it was the longest two hour drive I had ever made, I kept going over and over in my mind concerning the miracle that had taken place just two days before.

After spending four months of intense grieving and finely accepting the loss of my Mommy, both Dads, brother and two sisters, God was working another miracle. On March 18, 1994, I went to Arkansas to try to get some information to find my brother. Using the wrong name of the town he lived in and his wrong first name, my persistent husband made a few phone calls and found my brother, Earvin. I was elated. With the little we had to work with, God did indeed perform a miracle.

Because of my soul wounds, which had left me with issues surrounding rejection and abandonment, I didn't know for sure what kind of reception I would be getting. My ego shot arrows of doubt and fears. Why hadn't he tried to find me? What if he didn't want a relationship? What if I was going to be rejected again? I didn't know it at the time, but he was having some of the same feelings.

I will never forget the day I saw my big brother. What a reunion that was. As I watched him come down the steps from the porch and as I got out of the car my heart was beating so fast I could hear it. By the time we embraced in the middle of his front yard, all fears were washed away by tears of joy. At the same time, I could feel such healing take place that can compare with nothing else that I had ever experienced. As we held each other, it was as if I could feel a warm healing oil being poured through the top of my head and slowly making its way through every cell in my body. My soul wounds were being healed. As we held each other and the tears of joy flowed, I knew first hand about miracles. I knew that God was allowing me to start to find some of what I had lost.

For the first time I met his thoughtful wife, Brenda and their three adult children. For the four short hours that we were together, we took pictures, cried and hugged a lot. They kept saying they weren't going to ever let me go again. My brother's grown children said they had heard about me as the "Aunt in Dallas" all their life. I fell in love with them immediately. I left there with so much love; feelings of being special to someone, having roots, and that I belonged. I left there knowing that I was part of a family. I left learning that our Mommy's name is Gracie, which reminds me of God's grace which had made all this possible. My sister in law had even put together a box of pictures for me during the years. She also sent me home with a clipping from her pink rose bush and a rabbit, which she had made just for me. It's dressed in pink and looks great on my bed. They said that Daddy always talked about finding me and when he got sick in 1978 and was told he didn't have long to live, he said he wasn't going to die until he saw his baby girl one more time. That was when his family started looking for me. They sent for a Dallas telephone book and started calling all the Browns listed. There are lots of pages of Browns and they could only afford to call so many each month. The next step on their agenda was to get information about the Missing Persons show on television. On the evening I called them I started to tell my sister in law who I was and she said, "I know who you are and we have been expecting you to call."

It was in the fall of 1992, after being in therapy for about three months, that I wanted to find my brother. I had sent a letter to the town I thought he lived in, but it was returned. On November 5, 1992, during my therapy session, I was grieving the loss of both my Daddies and the fact that I had to grow up with out one. I found out later that our Daddy had died October 31, 1992. I can see God's wisdom in not allowing me to find my brother because then I would have found Daddy only to have to lose him again. Yet God had provided a way to grieve losing him. Yes, I believe in miracles.

Brother and I share both parents. He is seven years older than I. I finally have a big brother and I, at the age of fifty, was the baby sister. I can't tell you the joy I felt when he called me his baby sis.

Then God did it again. I had also left brother's that day with phone numbers and addresses of my two older half sisters. Rosie Lee lives in Arkansas about two hours from brother and Birtha Mae lives in Kalamazoo, Michigan. We share the same loving Mom which is really special. For some reason I had never allowed myself to even dream of finding my sisters. Maybe I had the fear that they were not alive or that maybe they wouldn't want to see me.

After all these years, not knowing these people, it was really hard to find the courage to take the risk of being rejected and write them. I was so afraid they might not would want a relationship. After all they didn't take me to raise after Mommy died. That was another loss I had grieved not knowing the circumstances. Somewhere I found the courage and wrote a week or so later and I shared all these fears. I received more than I could have imagined. Just like me they had suffered their own grief of losing me.

Rosie Lee received her letter first and called me. Her family had been searching for me for years, also. She is nineteen years older than I. She gave me a lot of information about our Mom. She loved me and wanted to see me. We cried a lot. I immediately felt the love for and from my big sister. Again, I knew I was experiencing another miracle.

The next day I received a call from my sister Birtha Mae's daughter, Judy. It was a most emotional time. She said she wanted to talk to me first to let me know how much her Mom loved me. She had always talked about me and they, too had been searching for me. She said because Birtha had wanted to take me after our Mommy died, but Dad thought I would be better off being adopted by the Wests, she had grieved all these years. She had not spoken to Dad for over forty years, until just before he died. She said there had been times when her Mom just felt that something was wrong and that I needed her. She grieved because she didn't know where I was so she could help me. There were times she thought about me and cried.

When Birtha and I finally got to talk, we had a hard time because we were both crying so hard. She talked about how this was an answer to a lot of prayers. She, being seventy three, had told God she didn't care if she had to live to be 150 she didn't want to die until she could see me one more time. I'm still asking God to allow her to live until she is 150 so we can have the next seventy two years to love each other. I could feel all this love that I had missed gently washing over me as we cried tears of joy. God is so good. We started making plans for a family reunion in Arkansas for the middle of July. Yes, I believe in miracles.

For nearly four months we wrote and talked on the phone. As the time got closer, I was more nervous. They could still choose not to like me or accept me. I talked to God a lot so these fears would not rob me of the joy I knew He had in store for us.

On Wednesday, July 14, 1994, two years to the day when I had my first therapy session with Dr. K., I received a different kind of therapy, a different kind of healing. After over forty eight years my sister Rosie and I held each other and cried. The last time she had held me there were tears of grief. Now they had been replaced with tears of joy. Yes, I believe in miracles.

She taught me how to play Skip-O, we peeled peaches to make peach cobbler, we sung while her daughter Mary and Rosie's husband, Sidney played the guitar, and we held each other every chance we got. We had about twenty four hours to get acquainted and learn about each other before Birtha and some of her family arrived.

I was not prepared for what they brought with them that Thursday late afternoon. As they piled out of the van, I had never experienced so much holding, not just hugging, but holding. Again, I could feel healing taking place as I experienced all the touching, holding and loving that they gave. It was like no one wanted to let go of the other. We just wanted to hold each other forever. It was like we were experiencing God's unconditional love and acceptance through each other.

As I watched the video a couple of weeks later and saw me touching, caressing, and stroking those I held, I realized how starved I had been for that safe touch. I realized I had to make sure it was real and that I wasn't dreaming. Through their touch I was being bathed in love.

With Birtha, came her husband, Ervin, who use to bounce me on his knee. His nickname was Peg Leg because he only had one good leg. I felt so safe with him as he held me. Also, her oldest daughter, Ann, who is about my age and her husband Jerry. If Sis had taken me, Ann and I would have grown up as sisters. Sis's youngest daughter, Judy, who is a year older than my oldest daughter, came with her husband, Don. I was so happy their husbands were there to experience this miracle too. Though Judy and Ann are my nieces, I feel close to them like sisters. We all have so much in common.

God still wasn't finished. He added so much to all this by including Judy and Don's little miracle, eight year old Mandy. This precious little jewel absolutely stole my heart and the heart of my inner child. We had never been happier as we played, raced, turned cartwheels, and giggled and giggled and giggled. She will never know what a healing was performed by our playing. We share a love for books, for sunsets, for skies, picture taking, and fun. She is wise beyond her years. She told me how lucky she felt being her Mom and Dad's little girl. I knew that she knew she was loved and I felt so happy for her. I knew I sure did love her. Yes, I believe in miracles.

My heart was really touched when Birtha said she had something for me that she had kept for nearly fifty years. I had no idea what it could be until she laid this folded yellowed tattered tiny baby dress in my hands. As I carefully held this little dress so afraid it would fall apart in my hands because of it's age and how delicate it was, I cried. I'm still not sure what the feelings were as Birtha was saying that this was the only thing that she had all these years that was a part of me. She had kept it all this time saying that when she found me she would give it back to me. I asked her if she was sure she wanted to part with it and she said, "Honey it's yours now. I was keeping it for you until I could give it to you. I don't need it any longer because I have you back." Yes, I believe in miracles.

Later, on one of our visits, Judy shared with me how there were times her Mom would take out the little dress and sat crying as she held and caressed it. Judy and her brothers and sisters knew not to bother their Mom at those times.

On Friday morning Judy, Ann, and Mandy brought flowers to us three sisters. Mandy chose to present me mine along with a big hug. In with the beautiful carnations was a single pink rose bud which Mandy had insisted on including. I know she had no idea of my love for pink roses so yes, I believe in miracles.

To my sisters' families, I'm still Aunt Rosa Mae. I had found out that Birtha was the one who named me. Even before I was born she told our Mom that I was going to be a girl and she wanted to name me. Our Mom asked her what she wanted to name me and she said, "Rosa Mae." I was named after both my big sisters.

The reunion was fantastic. My brother can fry the best catfish you ever put in your mouth. (As someone mention, he could have fried bologna sandwiches and I would have been just as pleased.) It was such a blessing to have my birth family together. I had never dreamed of having a family reunion with my side of the family. It's like God absolutely out did Himself this time. Yes, I believe in miracles.

Later in the afternoon Jim and I joined the group from Michigan and we toured Graceland in Memphis.

Afterward, we met back at Rosie's house to enjoy some music. Some of her children had gotten together with guitars, a banjo, and a mandolin for some down home pickin' and singing. This was a special treat. One of the songs that we joined Mary in singing was "Amazing Grace." Even amongst the clatter in the kitchen, the noise and laughter of the children, it was as beautiful and angelic as if a choir of angels were singing it. I think for a few minutes time stood still and even the angels were quiet as we lifted our voices in thanksgiving. For a few moments the cares, pains, and problems of life were put on hold. Yes, in those moments we believed in miracles.

Again, I could feel such a healing take place. I can't begin to describe in words what this was like. The void was being filled. The safe love and acceptance of family that I grew up without, but had searched for all these years, even as an adult child, I found in the arms of my brother, sisters and their warm loving families. It was like I was remembering when they had held me the first year and a half of my life. I was relearning what I had forgotten, but all the time my soul needed so badly. Because of the time together, we have started making memories that will live in our hearts forever.

One of the first things I found out with all the picture taking was that I'm taller than both my big sisters. Being five feet three, there's not many people that I'm taller than except maybe my grandchildren who are about to catch up with me. So this was an exciting thing to find out and to tease with. By the time our weekend was over, I was answering to Rosa Mae as fast as I was to Lorraine.

I guess the hardest thing to hear was, "good bye, Aunt Rosa Mae." But you know, God worked another miracle. Though it was sad to let go when our time together was finished, there was so much joy because we were so thankful for the miracle He had performed by bringing us together. There was so much joy because we knew we were one day closer to seeing each other again. We were one day closer to holding each other and experiencing this phenomenal miracle over and over again.

Before, I had felt sad and grieved the fact that I missed out on a lot of things by not growing up with my siblings. As we talk on the phone, since we have been home, we have come to the agreement that though it would have been great to grow up together, God had His own reasons for letting us wait all these years to find each other. We would not want to change anything. We have gotten to experience miracles that most people only get to read about. It seems, for different reasons, we all needed these miracles in our lives at this time. We have all had needs met. We have all been touched in some way. With gratefulness we end each phone conversation and each correspondence with, "we're one day closer to being together again." Yes, I believe in miracles.

Doesn't it seem exactly like a "God Deal" that two years from the day I started my recovery journey I started another new chapter in my life? I have started another new beginning. Some of what I had lost and grieved for, He didn't just replace, but actually gave it back to me. He has replaced the pain and grief of the past with joy and love for today. I'm reminded of a scripture found in 2nd Corinthians 5:17 reading, *"old things are passed away; behold and all things are become new."* Yes, I believe in miracles.

(Since the above was written, Peg Leg made his transition in December of '95. I'm so thankful I was able to spend some time with him before he left. He taught me about talking on the CB and gave me the Handle "Dusty Rose." I gave him a haircut and shared in his having fun when we drove up to the Indian Reservation to play the slots. I'm thankful for the memories we made.)

Section Two

My Poems: God's Gift To Me, My Gift To You

I Love the Smells of Thanksgiving Day

November 22, 1992

I love the smells of Thanksgiving Day.
The smell of fresh cut grass and home grown roses have been replaced.
Now we enjoy the aroma of the turkey in the smoker
and the fire in the fireplace.

I love the smells of Thanksgiving Day.
Which smell do you like the best or is it a tie?
Is it the sweetness of cloves and cinnamon from the pumpkin pie
or the pungent sage in the dressing that puts the twinkle in your eye?

I love the smells of Thanksgiving Day.
When you have freshly shaven gents with after shave
and ladies with their cologne.
There is no need for potpourri or room air spray

I just love the smells of Thanksgiving Day.

My Anger

January 15, 1993

I'm angry at the circumstances that kept my needs for love, attention, and affection from being met.
Instead, it was the hands of uncles, cousins, and neighbors all over me that became the only attention I could get.
I'm angry for the confused feelings as my young body responded to their touch,

But how is a little girl to know that this is not the kind of attention she needs so much?

I'm angry that my innocence and purity were taken from me at such an early age.
My feelings of fear, shame, guilt, and sadness were repressed, even the rage.

I'm angry at the circumstances, for whatever reason, that took my caretakers away.
They weren't there to protect me and I was afraid to trust them with what I needed to say.

I'm angry that it wasn't bad enough to go through the pain and torment of the abuse itself,
But I still have to endure the pain again and again as I work on freeing my child within of the secrets I've kept.

I'm angry that for all these years, without knowing it, and all alone, I've carried the guilt and shame.
It's taken lots of work and love for myself and the child within to learn it wasn't our fault. We're not to blame.

I'm angry that while my life was being torn apart at the seams and I would have welcomed death with open arms,
Those sorry spineless bastards were walking around free as a bird and still hurting others with no fear or alarm.

I'm angry that I didn't know before they died and went to their just reward,
But then, I'm reminded by someone very special to me,
"Vengeance is mine," saith the Lord.

There's Joy in Healing

January 21, 1993

There is joy in
healing, don't you know.
With each new person
you share, more joy will grow.

From every new
memory and feeling you relive,
that's more love for yourself
and the child within you can give.

For each new
feeling that you feel,
that's more
courage you receive to heal.

Each high and
low you struggle through
brings you closer
to the stronger new you.

For every day you
endure the healing pain,
that's one less day
you'll have to feel the shame.

There is joy in
healing, don't you know?
Remember, it's how far
you've come, not how far to go.

How Do You Say Thanks?

January 29, 1993

How do you say thanks to that person who right from the start,
made you feel safe, secure, and trusting
tho you came in with a wounded heart?

How do you say thanks to that person that helps you
muddle through those first feelings of confusion and fears.
She teaches you about feelings, gives you permission to feel
and you experience the cleansing while crying all those tears?

How do you say thanks to that person,
who after hearing about your abuse and its shame,
Keeps telling, keeps assuring, keeps saying over
and over, "It's not your fault, you're not to blame?"

How do you say thanks to that
concerned person that takes the extra time
to return phone calls when you're in a
panic, or reads your letters, journals, and rhymes?

How do you say thanks to that person
that understands the stages you're going through
And is there to calmly encourage and
challenge with suggestions of things to try and do?

How do you say thanks to that person that
spent countless hours reading, studying, and learning
to teach you to embrace the challenge to change while
a new passionate commitment within your heart is burning?

How do you say thanks to that person
that you feel closer to than a best friend,
but you know one day you'll be well
and your times with her will have to end?

How do you say thanks to that person
that you've never hugged or touched?
The only way I know is to say, "I appreciate you more
than you'll ever know, Dr. K. and I love you so very much."

Closed Doors

February 22, 1993

As you're traveling down the road of life looking
for an open door and there is none as you had supposed,
Just walk up to one and start knocking, you'll never
know what treasure may be behind a door that is closed.

It may feel a little scary
to take a risk or a chance,
but you'll never know what golden nuggets you'll find,
your life to enhance.

So take a deep breath,
hold your head up high.
March up to that door
and get your piece of the pie.

My Secrets

March 10, 1993

We've got a secret.
I had to promise not to tell.
Good girls don't do
what I did or they'll go to hell.

Can't tell my mom.
She'll get mad and send me away.
Have to keep all these dark
secrets safe inside so I can stay.

Can't tell my best friends.
Who knows what they would do?
I wonder if they have dark
secrets that they can't talk about too.

If I can't tell anyone then I
have to push it farther down.
Deeper and deeper down inside
of me until no more room is found.

When I have secrets, I should
be able to laugh, giggle, and share.
But not this kind of secret. We can't
take the chance that anyone would hear.

Even if I could tell
someone, what would they think?
Probably that I made it up and
they would forget it before I could blink.

Maybe I did, maybe they're right
and maybe it didn't happen at all.
But if that's true, why do I feel scared and shaky.
Why do I want to throw up when my name he calls?

All these years I carried these
secrets along with the guilt and shame.
All these years I've been like a
wounded little girl not understanding the pain.

Now I'm an adult
and feel free as a bird.
I've pulled up the secrets one
by one until they've all been heard.

No more hidden secrets will
keep me in bondage and chains.
My life is happier and healthier since my
body, soul, and spirit has been reclaimed.

Life's Worth Living

May 30, 1993

I feel as if my dreams have
all turned into fearful nightmares.
I feel I've fallen from my boat of
hope into the murderous lake of despair.

My life has been filled with a
mixture of sadness, loneliness and pain.

I know there are good memories too,
but they just don't balance out the same.

In helplessness I've searched and
asked for someone to give me a clue.
Why do I want to keep fighting
to live, and they say, "do it for you."

It really doesn't make good
sense, try as hard as I can,
Why go on fighting to survive?
I guess I really don't understand.

What is really out there to make me
have a reason to fight another day?
I start and stop again and again.
Every time the pain keeps getting in the way.

They say, "don't think about tomorrow.
Just hang on and get through this day, this hour.
Keep on believing this too shall pass, the pain won't
last forever. You can make it through as God gives you power."

I guess I'm just weak and
tired from all the energy spent.
I want to lay down and
rest inside of a protective tent.

A tent made of love, compassion,
safety, healing and free of fear and pain.
No more betrayal, no more despair,
depression, and no more guilt and shame.

I cry out, "what is the real
reason to want to keep on living?
Is it to search for happiness or is
it true that I'll find happiness in giving?"

But to whom and what
do I have that is worth giving?
Again the question rings out with out an
answer clear, "what makes life worth living?"

Then deep inside a small quiet voice reminds me that
she coped through all the loneliness and the actual pain of the abuse.
She was the victim who became numbed without
feelings in order to become a survivor so that I could break loose.

What I've been experiencing is the
destructive damaging effects of the abuse and pain.
Now that it's clear, I too can learn to be a
survivor of the effects and learn to want to live again.

Now I know the answer to the questions.
I know what I can give and what I can share.
It's me, my experiences, an encouraging word
through my writings, poems, or maybe just a simple prayer.

Where do I find them and to whom
do I give these things so lovingly and free?
I look around and see that it's all the people
out there hurting. People just like you and me.

My Past

October 14, 1993

I want to choose the path of
less fear, sorrow, anger, and pain.
I know lots have traveled it.
Relief and quietude were their gain.

Tho others will not understand,
they'll hurt and be grievous, too
I can't think of them this time.
That's their stuff they'll have to work through.

I've done my working through the
best I could as long as I could find help.
But then there comes a time,
when I'm expected to do it all myself.

Well, I find it's just to damn much
for this "adult child" to handle all alone.
My nerve endings feel raw, are
all exposed and I feel bare to the bone.

I feel there is no one here with time
to listen. There's no one that can hear
the tormenting cries and the sorrowful
wailing as the past keeps drawing near.

It's upon me abruptly with the
same dreaded sickening fear and pain.
I can't get through the day without its
chilling face appearing again and again.

By no surprise, it's here in the night time
masked in nightmares and panic attacks.
It's in the sleeplessness, the cold
sweats, the trying to get my breath back.

I accept that it will always be here
to haunt me, to drive me slowly insane,
making the effort to live seem useless
and hopeless. I feel I'm losing at this game.

Painful feelings keep popping up
and I can't push them down any longer.
I just want to wave the white flag
in surrender because I'm not stronger.

I feel overwhelmed and defeated
in this bloodless battle for sanity.
Every endeavor seems to be for
nothing, just like with the rest of humanity.

I'm told it's best to feel the
pain, talk about it, and then let it go.
I wish it was as easy as it
sounded, or I wish I wasn't so slow.

It's only a matter of time before the
end will come and I can say good-bye.
Then I can quit trying to fight
to survive and just lay down and die.

I want to choose the path of
less fear, sorrow, anger and pain.
I know lots have traveled it.
Relief and quietude were their gain.

The Fork in the Road

October 22, 1993

I've come to a fork in the
road on this journey to recovery.
This is something I didn't know
about and could be a painful discovery.

I stand here and look as I'm
coming through a lot of pain and fear,
which way do I want to go?
Should I take this one or the one over there?

Can't see around the bend as
to what lies ahead on either one.
I do know one way will lead to
death and the other one will lead me on.

If I choose the one that leads to my
death and removes me from my pain,
would it be the best way to
go, my peace and tranquillity to gain?

Is the serenity that I find
there real or is it only a mirage?
Will I find that it is forever or
is it just temporally before my eyes?

It is a road frequently traveled.
One that there is no turning back.
There will be no changing my mind.
It will take me to a place that feels black.

It's a lonely place where no one
can go with me. I will be all alone.
It's a road to a place that once I
start, there will be no time to postpone.

I look at the other road and
what do I see facing me there?
I know there will always be
pain, but there's also others to share.

This road is wide enough for more than
one to travel side by side at the same time.
There will always be someone sharing
the journey with me and that's a good sign.

This road will never be lonely
and does not lead to forever blackness.
This road also has joy, peace, long
suffering, and is filled with loving kindness.

Sometimes it may not be easy to
continue on knowing there is still pain before me,
but it makes it worth while knowing
what lies ahead at the end of this journey.

I guess when I sit back and look at
my two choices that are waiting before me,
I have, with gratitude in my heart, to
choose the one that allows me to help others to see.

I know there are others taking this
same journey on their way to their recovery.
I want them to see the only way is to choose
the fork in the road that leads them to their self discovery.

This is truly the only one that can
bring happiness both now and forever.
This is the way to lead us home
to live forever with our Lifegiver.

My Prayer of Thanksgiving

November 25, 1993

How do we say thanks, Father, for our
loving, happy, growing family gathered round?
No richer more significant blessing than
this under heaven or on this earth can be found.

You have gloriously added to it this year by giving us Baby
Jake and reminding us of not just the miracle of birth, but the
miracle of life.
But you didn't stop there, Father, You brought more joy and
love into our hearts by giving Lisa to David for his loving wife.

How do we say thanks, Father, for day after
day you keep us healthy, safe and out of harms' way?
Your blessed protectiveness is continually covering
and reminding us that you are with us both night and day.

How do we say thanks, Father, for providing us
with jobs to pay for the necessities and the meeting of our needs?
None of us have been hungry, without clothes, had
to sleep in the cold, and somehow the bills manage to get paid.

How do I say thanks, Father, for the fullness of
your love that I feel and know that is deep within?
You've given me courage, wisdom, and strength
to look inside, to learn to love and accept who I am.

It's with this same thankfulness that I look at my family:
my husband who loves, tries to understand and tolerates,
My wonderful grandchildren who brings such joy and
laughter, my own cherished children, and their devoted mates.

How do we say thanks, Father, for your unconditional
love and acceptance of us, even with all our imperfections?
Could it be by doing the same for others. Learning to
overlook faults, differences and loving without conditions?

How do we say thanks, Father, for the most phenomenal gift
of all when you sent your willing Son to show us how to live?
What better way for us to say thanks than to look at others
less fortunate, maybe alone, and ask ourselves what can we give?

It may be nothing big or spectacular, may not be seen by anyone
but You. Yet to someone at that time, it could matter much.
It may be just a kind word, a helping hand, an understanding
nod, a smile, a hug, or just a warm comforting touch.

Maybe the best gift we can give back
and the way we can say thanks, Father,
Is to leave a little of your love everywhere
we go by being kind and loving to one another.

Who is This Therapist of Mine?

She is........
December 27, 1993

Someone who has been such a
significant part of my life for a year and a half.

She has been there with me with
my tears and frequently to share a laugh.

Someone whose good and bad
sides I've seen like a mother.
This lesson taught me that
one goes along with the other.

Someone I yearn to be best
friends with, sit and talk over coffee.
Have a chance to learn about
her instead of always talking about me.

Someone I would love to adopt as my
sister with whom I could do special sisterly things.
These are treasures that are worth
more to me than gifts from Kings and Queens.

Someone I've learned from and
solicited approval from as my teacher.
The wisdom she has imparted has
been life changing, thus I'm so much richer.

Someone who listened and because
of that, I felt worthy to be listened to.
This was the beginning step to start
changing and making my life brand new.

Someone who taught me to use the power
within to learn and make necessary changes.
That my life didn't have to stay the same
and that life is compiled of many different stages.

Someone who introduced me to my
extraordinary courageous little children within.
I was able to learn to become their
loving mother as well as make them my friends.

Someone who encouraged me to not
fear the feelings whether they be joy or pain.
It was only through the feeling that I
could ever hope to let go of the guilt and shame.

Someone who was there to comfort
and say, "I'm sorry" in the midst of my pain.
I'm learning to feel, grieve, and let go.
My life, thank God, will never be the same.

Someone who taught me to see there
is good and bad in all of us and it's okay.
Loving and accepting others and our
selves unconditionally is the only true way.

Someone who taught me I could make
my own choices as well as I had other rights.
This is knowledge that will be forever
etched in my heart as I walk in this new light.

Someone who taught me that it was okay to
make mistakes, just take the responsibility for them.
No longer will I let perfection stand in my
way for fear of mine or someone else's criticism.

Someone who reminded me I was
stronger and look how far I'd come.
All I have to do is look at the battles I
have fought and the victories I have won.

Someone who helped renew my love for books,
thirst for learning, and my search for knowledge.
I know it is this inner hunger and the
continual wanting to grow that will give me the edge.

Someone who helped me to see the hidden
treasures within me that had been hidden so deep.
I feel like a fairy princess who, with a
kiss, has been awakened from a long deep sleep.

Someone who guided me to search for the
real me. I no longer have to live as my false self.
No longer do I have to do and say what
I'm supposed to or try to be like everybody else.

Someone who I love and have to lose, not
by divorce or by death, which I feel would be easier.
It's just one of those necessary losses that is
part of life that somehow will make me healthier.

Someone who's going to be there one minute,
but the next she's going to be gone, yet she's not.
She will never be that far from me because
no one can take her nor my memories from my heart.

Normal

January 21, 1994

Normal, God I wish I was normal,
whatever the heck normal really is.
How do you know how normal looks
or can you tell me how normal feels?

Normal, whose to say what it looks like
because we each see through different eyes.
Normal, whose to say what normal feels like
because we're as different as the stars in the sky.

Normal can not be modeled or mirrored
by people like him, her, them, me or you.
Normal is our own responses and reactions
to the experiences that we have been through.

Normal, we are all completely
normal each in our own special unique way.
Our normal, just like each
snowflake, is different, but our difference is okay.

Time

January 23, 1994

Time is passing quickly from me like
snowflakes melting before hitting the ground.
Where do the days, hours, minutes, and
seconds go. I can't find them anywhere around.

They were here just a little while ago
when I was young and everything was new.
Now they have disappeared, forever
gone, never again to be seen by me or you.

Time takes with it the laughter and
innocence of the child that is now grown up.
Time brings with it the tears for things
and people that I loved, but had to give up.

Time takes with it the energy and
the desire to live happily ever after.
Time brings with it the loneliness
and the yearning for children's laughter.

Time takes with it my health,
beauty, vitality and little pieces of my mind.
Time brings with it only those precious
memories of things and people left behind.

Time for most of us is seemingly to
short, just seventy or eighty years or so.
Half of that is spent in living other
people's lives and advising them of what we know.

A fourth of that is spent living,
being, and doing what we really want to do.
The other fourth is spent our being the
child and our children helping us get through.

It appears that the older and
busier we get the faster time seems to fly.
There just isn't time to do all the
things we want before its our time to die.

In just three short weeks from now
I'll be turning fifty and "over the hill."
I've been richly blessed with newness
of life and lots of new creative skills.

Life just seems to be getting better
and better with each passing day.
I just can't ask for more than
this. Nothing can stand in my way.

I know that we are not
promised another day after this one,
so I plan to live it full steam
ahead and have lots more fun.

I want to help others along the
way that need my love and support.
While here on this earth, in the
time of storms, I can be that safe port.

Time is flying by faster than a
speeding bullet sailing through the air.
We can't waste a minute. Live life to
the fullest, and let others know we care.

My Sleepless Nights

January, 1994

Was it something that I ate
that's making me lie here wide awake?
I think not or I would get
up and some Rolaids I would take.

Maybe, by chance it's what's
eating me that causes my mind to swirl.
There's just to many things going
on inside my head, my heart, my world.

With thoughts and feelings,
like a whirlwind or tornado in my head,
it's impossible to close my eyes
in sleep no matter how long I've been in bed.

Tossing, turning, and watching
the numbers slowly change on the clock,
are mindless things to do
as I look inside myself and take stock.

For a few weeks now, I've
stuffed the feelings of pain as not to show
the loneliness, helplessness and
hopelessness that I've come to know.

When can I find the peaceful
rest from all this pain and sorrow?
When can I close my eyes in
sleep and wake up fresh on the morrow?

Maybe tomorrow night after
a warm relaxing candle lit bubble bath,
I can lay on my fresh clean
sheets and slumber without all this wrath.

I'll have a cup of warm
milk laced with sugar and cinnamon.
As I swallow I can feel it
washing away some of the poisonous venom.
As my eye lids become heavy with sleep,
I'll pray the Lord my soul to keep.

Death's Arms

February 27, 1994

It was death's unmerciful arms
that to soon snatched my Mommy away

before I had the chance to know
her, love her, and before we had time to play.

It was death's arms that so
hardheartedly stripped my childhood from me,
leaving me abandoned, my Daddy
and brother I would never again get to see.

Death's unrelenting arms took my new
Daddy away before our dreams became real.
Then all of the old wounds were reopened
before they had a chance to completely heal.

Is it any wonder, some fifty years later, I'm
still looking for what I was given, but was taken.
It was indeed a cruel callous thing that
was done and has left my foundation badly shaken.

Is it then a big surprise while in my search,
I found what I thought I longed for and needed,
In the enveloping arms of death itself
while all the knowledge I had, went unheeded.

With death's arms closing around me,
I thought I'd found the warmth I had yearned for.
I had found the closeness, the touching
and the release of pain that I'd not known before.

As I relaxed deeper into the strong arms
of death, knowing my struggling would be over soon,
I looked at those close to me who had no
idea of what I was feeling, not knowing of my doom.

I had tried to tell them. I tried to make
them understand the horrible grief and pain I was in.
But they either couldn't handle it, or they
were too busy. I just know, I wasn't being heard again.

Just as I was about to give up and close
my eyes for the last time for that final rest and sleep,
I heard a cry for help. Someone needed to
be rescued and somehow I knew it was left up to me.

I hesitated for a moment in my fear, not
sure I wanted to leave these enfolding arms so secure.
Then I heard the faint cry again. It was the
sound of a little child's voice so innocent, soft and pure.

It wasn't just one voice, but many that were
crying out in their grief and pain seemingly all alone.
It was then I had to break away from death's
grip that had suddenly become chilling to the bone.

As I set out to find these hurting people to
give them hope and help to survive to carry through,
The small voice of my own child within said,
"Thank you for listening, I knew I could count on you."

I learned through this that it is purpose
that gives us the joy, the strength to survive each day.
Taking one day at a time, reaching out to
others, is the hope for our survival. It's the only way.

Now I have left the passionless arms of
death with all its false securities and promises of harm.
I'm safe and secure in my faith of the power
within while being cradled in GOD'S sheltering arms.

Life's Contrasts

March 3, 1994

I see that life is made up
of joy and pain,
losses and gains,
sunshine and rain,

the good and the bad,
the happy and the sad,

the new and the old,
the scared and the bold,

the love and the hate,
the hurry up and wait,

the need to laugh
and the need to cry,
the wanting to live
and the wanting to die,

the miracle and joy of birth
and the grief of death,
the ungrateful and those
thankful for each breath,

exciting new beginnings
and sorrowful endings,
open arms welcoming,
and farewells and partings,

those who are weak
and those who are strong,
those who moan and groan
and those with a song,

those wanting to give
and those wanting to take,
those who follow and those
whose own way they make,

those who hold it in
and those who share,
those who care not
and those who care,

those who are needy
and those who meet their needs,
those who reap
and those who plant the seeds,

those who build up
and those who tear down,
those who are serious
and those who clown around.

I see life as contrasts.
We experience not one or the other,
but a combination of all of
them working, in us, together.

I see life is not all good or bad or
is it all black or white, but really gray.
We aren't perfect or imperfect, but
are to do our best in what we do or say.

I see that life is made up
of joy and pain,
losses and gains,
sunshine and rain.

Life's a Game

March 3, 1994

I see that life is forever
changing, nothing staying the same.
Change is good they say.
Personally I see life as just a game.

It"s not whether we lose or
win that counts, but it's how we play.
The significant thing to remember
is that in this contest, we need to stay.

In this rugged game there
are no spectators only us players.
There are no judges, no
referees, umpires or arbitrators.

We are on the same team
and eventually learn to play together.
We can't do it by ourselves,
we need and depend on each other.

The rules of the game are
pretty much the same for everyone.
When the ball is in our court,
we make the choice to stay or run.

We can look at the circumstances
that affect us and choose to take flight
or we can look at them squarely,
gather our courage, stand up and fight.

We can forever live and
dwell in our pain, grief, and sadness
wishing for things to have
been different and feeling no gladness.

Or we can choose to take the
ruins, the ugly horrible things of our past
and learn to make of them
something beautiful, something that will last.

Which ever choice we make,
it's ours. We must accept all responsibilities.
No one can take that from us,
therefore we have innumerable possibilities.

As participants we don't have
to rely on just our knowledge and insight.
We have the authority to ask God
for Wisdom, which He gives with delight.

This is much better than home field
advantage, rabbit's feet, or four leaf clovers.
If we make a mistake and mess up,
He just smiles and allows us to have "overs."

It isn't necessary to depend or
trust on our human strength alone.
For God has freely given us
His power to use on our journey home.

*One day this game will end and
we will receive our prize our reward.
It will all depend on how well
we played, not on how well we scored.*

*Therefore, it is to our advantage
to make every play count and give it our best.
Then, with contentment in our
soul, we see God's Grace as He makes up the rest.*

Life is Precious

March 14, 1994

*I feel like a small child
turned loose in a candy store
getting to sample pieces
of life and wanting more.*

*I want to taste it all, the sweetness
of good and the bitterness of the bad.
Then sample something
else to see if it's better than the other I had.*

*For so long I had been
denied this simple pleasure,
now life to me is like
a wonderful hidden treasure.*

*Really enjoying and
living this incredible life
is such an adventure
even with the pain and strife.*

I now know the awesome
difference between existing and living.
This revelation came to me
when I was taught about feeling.

For all these years it's like
I have been in a robotic trance
marching to the beat of someone
else's drum, afraid to take a chance.

Now I've been liberated,
I'm at peace, I've been set free.
No longer will the bonds of
self doubt and fear hinder me.

It's taken lots of work, lots
of crying and lots of praying.
But it has been worth it all
just for this poem to be sharing.

Though I have always loved
and trusted God even in the past,
it's now that I'm experiencing
the kind of faith that I know will last.

I guess it's when you
almost accidentally loose something,
that it becomes more
valuable and precious than anything.

For this new life, it seems my days
are filled with a constant thanksgiving.
I find that my mortal words seem
so inadequate for the privilege of living.

I know that He understands
and knows what I'm trying to say.
I just want to love Him, thank
Him and share Him along the way.

Life is so precious, so full, so rewarding, and
so abundant, I never again want to take it for granted.
Because I know the Lifegiver who has given
me life so freely, I know this is the way He planned it.

I Talked to Mom West

March 16, 1994

I sat down and had a talk
with Mom West yesterday.
For the first time I could
tell her what I wanted to say.

I could never do that while
growing up because of the fear.
But yesterday I got to tell
her what I wanted her to hear.

It was hard because I had never
before talked to her about feeling.
I knew it was a big step that I had
to take. It was part of my healing.

Once I started, both the words and
healing tears flowed at the same time.
It was then that I knew it was okay.
I wasn't committing some awful crime.

I told her of the sadness I felt for
her because of the hardness of her life.
I felt sad because she had no
gentleness, not much joy, but lots of strife.

I felt sad because the wall of
protection she had built all around
also kept out the people that
loved her since no way in could be found.

Because of her protective wall
she could not touch, hug, or be close.
We that loved her suffered, but I
think she's the one that suffered the most.

She must have been hurt badly
sometime in her life to have such fear.
I wish she could have talked to me
and shared her story so I could hear.

I told her how hard it was to
live with her critical side which I hated.
I could never please her. I felt
low on the scales with which she rated.

I told her of the insecurities I felt
wondering if she would send me away
if I messed up one time to many
or if the wrong thing I might do or say.

This is how I learned to act, do and
say what I thought everyone else wanted.
With no feelings, thoughts, or opinions
of my own, my adult life has been haunted.

I talked to her about the beatings and
what I learned from her about venting anger.
Anger brought yelling, screaming, physical
and emotional pain and red flags of danger.

Stay away from confrontations at all cost
because I never knew where they would lead.
I might lose control, become a mad woman,
and for their life someone might have to plead.

I could never imagine in my wildest
dreams of inflecting such pain on someone I loved.
Therefore I must have been unloved,
unwanted, no good, etc.... All these feelings, I shoved.

Through my healing, because of my growing and
my feeling, I choose to look at things differently now.
Not excusing what mom did, but I know she worked
with the knowledge she had and did the best she knew how.

She chose to adopt, take care of my
physical needs, and raise me as her own.
Even though before the adoption was
final, Daddy West died and left us alone.

She worked hard all by herself from sun up
to sun down running the little country store,
keeping the farm with the animals going,
seemingly content, not asking for anything more.

Later when I was ten mom had to sell
everything we had and we moved to town.
It seemed she had to work harder and
when I needed her protection she was not around.

Though she wasn't there for me
emotionally to give the loving touching I so craved,
She gave me her love in other ways
that I can see now and I don't feel so depraved.

I can look at her now and admire her
strength, her backbone, and her steadfastness.
I know I gained so much from her. Old
fashion values like honesty, integrity, and goodness.

She taught me about God. I learned that
He was our Provider. Everything was His own.
From those seeds, lovingly planted and
nurtured while young, my faith today has grown.

Because of my healing, I feel such love,
acceptance, compassion and forgiveness.
First for myself, but especially for Mom,
along with understanding and gratefulness.

Though I didn't receive this knowledge
and feel these feelings before she passed on,
I feel assured that one day face to face I'll
tell her when I join her in our heavenly home.

I feel with the writing of this poem that Mom's
protective wall is no longer needed and is finally torn down.
We are both free to love and forgive each other.
The love I've searched for all these years has been found.

In Loving Memory of my Mom

Scars

March 17, 1994

Some have scars on the outside
caused by a cut or being burned.
Some have scars on the inside
because their life was over turned.

In either case the
effects can be seen by all.
Some scars are huge
while others are small.

Whether they are
underneath or on the surface,
they came from a hurt,
a wound, or a pain in either case.

The surface wounds
heal and leave a reminder.
The wounds on the
inside may take a little longer.

The healing from the scars
themselves starts coming
when we learn to accept
who we are and stop blaming.

When we learn to stop trying
to cover them up and hide them,
the freedom comes and our cup
of happiness is filled to the brim.

True beauty must
always come from deep within
so it only makes sense
that's where healing begins.

Whether it's scars on
the inside or on the outside,
the thing to remember is
behind them don't try to hide.

The Color Gray

March 17, 1994

The color gray has
become a symbolic color to me.
First I learned just black
or white, it doesn't have to be.

It doesn't have to be good
or bad, sunshine or rain that splatters.
It's all the wonderful things in
the middle that are real, that matters.

Even with the beautiful dark
gray clouds with their promise of rain,
I know the sun is near by reminding
me that joy is also near when I'm in pain.

There's also the beautiful gray skies
just before the dawning of each new day.
I'm reminded that each day is a new
beginning and the yesterdays have passed away.

*When my learning experiences for the day
are over, again the sky is gray with the dusk.
That's when I'm filled with regrets of things
not accomplished, or satisfaction of what was.*

*I guess the real blessing, of which I
was reminded when thinking of what to say,
was that my beautiful name given
to me at birth was Rosie Mae Gray.*

Gray Clouds

March 17, 1994

*I have learned something about the
beautiful soft gray clouds hanging in the sky.
There are the ones with silver, the
ones with blue, and all the others passing by.*

*When I see the dark gray clouds,
I know it's time for some refreshing rain.
Whether it's on a hot August day or
one in July, I welcome it with a joyful refrain.*

*I guess one of the prettiest sights
I ever saw was one day in the Spring.
The sun was shinning brightly and at
the same time it was pouring down rain.*

*The trees and the grass, even the sidewalks
glistened with the rain drops. Tho the sky was gray,
there was a brightness like a halo
around God's world as if to say, "everything is okay."*

It's a magnificent sight to see the sun peep
out from behind the gray clouds high in the sky.
Seeing the rays of sunlight playing in
the heavens, I know a rainbow must be near by.

I'm also reminded by someone very
special to me that the sun is always shinning.
It may be hid behind those beautiful gray
clouds, but it will soon come out from hiding.

There's something entirely different about
the fluffy marshmallow clouds in a sky of blue.
It's like the days when everything is
going great and all is well with the world and you.

Something stirs deep inside of me when I
see the sky with the ominous clouds of gray.
I think of newness of life, growth, and the
promise that better things are on their way.

I use to think of only the frightening storms
those clouds might bring with costly destruction.
It's a fact of life that storms do come. It's
at that time I know to seek God for His instructions.

Just like God sending the rainbow as a
promise to the generations after Noah and his family,
He has sent a beautiful rainbow into my
heart to remind me that He will always be with me.

I choose now to see these majestic gray
clouds as not a warning of an impending storm,
but instead a reminder that through the
storms of life, God is with me until He takes me home.

God's Gifts of Life and Choice

March 28, 1994

The gift of life He chose to give
me, not demanding anything in return.
Then He gave me the gift of choice
to share or not to share of what I learn.

This gift of choice certainly brings with it
certain responsibilities and special rewards.
The knowledge I gain from mistakes made and
the joy for a job well done is like my life's safety cord.

He even gave me the choice to believe
and trust Him to be my guide through this life.
Through the spirit of adoption, He became my
Heavenly Father and one day I will become His Son's wife.

I don't have to understand how all this works.
This is His world that I'm privileged to be a part.
I just know a lot of extraordinary miraculous things
happen because I believe, trust and love Him with all my heart.

I think even the trust, faith and
love I'm privileged to feel and know
are also gifts of His abiding
love that He so generously bestows.

I'm thankful for this phenomenal gift of life
because in all reality it's really not mine, but His.
I just choose to be a vessel and allow Him
to live through me so that others He may bless.

His Resurrection Gives Us Security

April 2, 1994

I'm thinking on this, the
eve of Easter Sunday morning,
of the first Easter long
ago and all those in mourning.

Their beloved teacher,
counselor, friend, the mighty Son of God
had been betrayed, mocked,
whipped, spat upon and then crucified.

I'm sure the pain of their loss was
immeasurable as their tears of sorrow flowed.
Their grief could not be contained as
they remembered the love He had bestowed.

This pain clouded their minds and
made them forget that just a short time before,
He told them this was going to happen.
In a little while and He would be with them no more.

Soon they would remember because
they would find the stone to His tomb rolled away.
They would remember He said that
He would die, but would rise again in three days.

Then He would ascend back to Heaven to
wait for all of us there with our Heavenly Father.
He has not left us here alone for He would
live in each one of us by His Spirit, our Comforter.

This was all part of God's marvelous
perfect plan to give us life eternal with Him.
Because of His love for us, He sent His
Son to die so we could have a home with them.

This eternal life doesn't start when
we close our eyes in death sometime in the future,
But it begins the moment we choose
to believe and trust, that in Him we become a new creature.

Because of our pain, sadness and grief, our mind
may become clouded and we might forget His reassuring promise.
In love He will remind us that because He now lives
within, we are secure in Him. He will never never leave or forsake us.

Resurrection From Within

April 3, 1994

I'm thinking, as I sit here on this beautiful Easter
Sunday morning, of the Resurrection that has taken place in my life.
I feel a liberation, a releasing, like I've been revived,
rescued and delivered from the effects of my past pain and strife.

I feel like a new person, like a
new or a rebirth has taken place within.
I really feel that old things are passing
away and all things are becoming new again.

I feel so thankful, so grateful for the
internal and eternal changes taking place.
I know that it is because of God's tender
mercies and His unchanging amazing grace.

With this resurrection and changes being made,
come the feelings of abundant Love, Joy and Peace.
I wish for everyone this knowledge and these
feelings so from the struggles in their life, they could cease.

I know this is something other than just head
knowledge that one learns from hearing or reading.
I've learned from God Himself through feeling
the pain and learning to rely on Him for my healing.

Not only the healing from the past
with its horrible effects on my life today,
but the healing of things in my life to come.
I learned that choosing to change was the only way.

By choosing to look at the over all picture of
my life instead of a circumstance here and there,
I see that God is indeed in control not only of
my life, but the whole world. So what do I have to fear?

Having this knowledge and being reminded
that I have a purpose here on this earth is quite a revelation.
Is it any wonder then that I feel such joy because
of my spiritual awakening about this, my inner resurrection?

My Hell

April 9, 1994

I felt that the earth had opened up and
swallowed me and there I had cried and wailed.
With my teeth gnashing, being in torment, and
feeling hopeless, this pain became my living hell.

It is not at all as I had imagined,
in all my wildest dreams, that it would be.
Though I couldn't feel it at times,
I knew through it all, God was with me.

I found that this hell didn't have to
be eternal. It was only for a short season.
I guess it could have been longer, but
God smiled and said, "but for what reason?"

I could have been stuck there
forever in that endless torment and pain.
But God, through His matchless
grace, showed me a new life I could gain.

I only had to accept and embrace
this phenomenal gift He offered so freely.
It was the gift of Him loving
others and living His life through me.

It's with His joy, peace and hope
that I accept this marvelous gift of love.
I know He will not take it from me.
It will forever be mine, as His mysteries I solve.

I stand in awe at this knowledge of the Gift
of Grace and with the huge responsibility with which it comes.
Though I feel unworthy to have been chosen for this
task, with His Wisdom, I will do my best until He takes me
home.

Knowledge Brings Responsibility

April 9, 1994

The first knowledge I received,
on this journey to healing and recovery,
was that some changes would have to be
made as I entered this phase of my self discovery.

With this new knowledge came different
responsibilities that I would assume along the way.
Soon, it seemed there were old things I would have to
unlearn and new things to learn with each passing day.

With this new knowledge, I learned that this journey
would take commitment and lots of work on my part.
For changes to be made, I had counted the
cost, and I knew I wanted this with all my heart.

I learned about the roller coaster ride to
hell. I learned about the fear of the unknown.
I learned about taking risks, of taking
chances and of leaving my old comfort zone.

I learned about the chance of losing
the security of my family, friends, and home.

I learned about the differences of dark
loneliness and that of just wanting to be alone.

I learned that my needs and the children
within were to become the most important things in my life.
For all the years before it was everyone else
because I was someone's daughter, mother, and wife.

As my emotional healing and growth progressed
day after day, I noticed something new was taking place.
I was feeling more peace, joy, hope and love.
It was, as I was to learn later, a gift of God called Grace.

Even in the roughest of life's storms,
and in the depth of the tormenting pain,
through faith in God, and the wisdom He gave,
a calm assurance of the power within, I had gained.

This, as I was to learn later, was Spiritual
healing and growth that I had never known.
I was in awe as I experienced this gift and
felt so unworthy of the seeds that He had sown.

I felt some fear at the responsibility of this
incredible knowledge He had so graciously and freely chosen
to give.
I remember hearing, "to whom much is given,
much is required," but "what if I fail Him as this life I try to
live."

He reminded me to seek Him for wisdom
and knowledge and in all things do my very best.
Just be a willing vessel to allow Him to live
through me, and He would take care of the rest.

With the knowledge of this gift of the miracle
of Grace comes responsibility, that, can not be denied.
It may be rising at two in the morning to write
a poem, or to receive words for a book that He's inspired.

All He requires is that I'm willing to accept
the challenge of the responsibility of these marvelous love gifts.
Because He lives within and through me, my
joy and love overflows as upward my soul He tenderly lifts.

...And I Cry

April 11, 1994

I think of walking into her office one last time,
hearing her close the door behind me,
and I cry.

I think of the awkwardness of trying to thank her,
and realize there are no adequate words,
and I cry.

I think of all the doctors that I could have had, but God knew
who I needed and blest me with her,
and I cry.

I think of the courageous new life I have because
of the knowledge and wisdom she shared,
and I cry.

I look at the way God has worked through her
and am so thankful that she was willing,
and I cry.

I look at the healing and growing,
both emotionally and spiritually, that's taken place,
and I cry.

I remember the very first visit when right away
I knew I was in a safe place with a safe person,
and I cry.

I remember when I, with no feelings, told her my story.
I can still see the sadness and compassion on her face,
and I cry.

I remember my first spark of feeling
when she said, "I'm sorry that happened to you,"
and I cry.

I think of the way she gave me her love,
by reading my letters and all the extra time spent,
and I cry.

I think that I must be a valuable person for her to be willing
to spend so much extra time,
and I cry.

I think of the way she listened to me giving me the feeling
that I must be worth listening to,
and I cry.

I think of the way she embraced me with the expressions in
her eyes, her soft soothing voice, and her warm smile,
and I cry.

I think of the way she threw challenges at me,
not doubting for a minute that I would accept them,
and I cry.

I think of the way she saw the strength in me that I didn't see
and encouraged me to find it for myself,
and I cry.

I think of her teaching me about rights, choices,
and the responsibilities that follow,
and I cry.
I think of the fact that I never learned, while growing up,
about having to say good bye,
and I cry,

I see this as the final lesson in my spiritual growth, that is
her responsibility as my "Recovery Angel," to teach me.
and I cry.

I think of that last forty five minute hour passing to swiftly by
and our final time together is finished,
and I cry.

I think of when I walk back through her door that final time,
to face the world without her. I hear that door close behind me,
and I cry.

I'm aware that I don't feel afraid, dependent, clingy, depressed,
rejected, abandoned, that I need her, or that I'm going to die,
and I cry.

I see ahead of me mixed with the sufferings of life, adventurous
new beginnings to enjoy with the dawning of each new day,
and I cry.

I think as I embrace these feelings of sadness that I am so
thankful for them, because they are evidence that I love and
I am loved,
and I cry.

I see the extraordinary work of God's matchless
amazing Grace at work in my life,
and I cry.

The Reason

April 13, 1994

Not long into this painful yet joyous
journey of my incest recovery and healing,
I asked why did sick people have to hurt
little children and take away their feelings?

Why was such a terrible thing allowed to happen to
innocent, little children, that only wanted love and attention?
Why was their childhood robbed? Why was horrible
painful things done to them? Things that can not be
mentioned.

And what about the sickness that took my
Mommy away so prematurely leaving me with grief?
Why couldn't some wonder drug have been
discovered that would keep her from shriveling like a leaf?

Why do these life changing storms sneak
into our lives so unexpected and take us unawares?
Why are we expected to hang on, be strong,
keep the faith, and how do we know God really cares?

As I've grown, matured and healed, through
blind faith I learned to accept that God had a reason.
I don't have to understand the why no more
than I have to know why or how He changes the seasons.

I've learned that on this planet we all have a job to do.
Why else would He have given us our own special place?
Through the circumstances of life we learn how not to just cope
on our own, but to grow and mature in Him as He gives us Grace.

I've learned that this life is going to be filled sometimes
with suffering and pain, balanced with joy and gladness as well.
We can ask for His wisdom and knowledge to deal responsibly
with the situations that arise while on this planet we dwell.

Each time that we recognize we are powerless
over all of life's sorrowful circumstances that come our way,
we are gently reminded to turn it over to the God within
and listen to the little voice inside to hear what He has to say.

I guess if I was still looking for a reason for
this and that which happens, I need to look no longer.
I would have to see it as part of my spiritual
growth making the God within bigger and me stronger.

My Feelings

April 17, 1994

Feelings, just like our beautiful children,
who bring such joy, are a miraculous gift from God.
For so many years I was like a barren woman,
empty of this gift as through this life I trod.

*Then one day someone, after hearing the
painful accounts of my childhood abuse, of which I was numb,
told me she was so sorry that it had happened to me and
asked how I felt. Then I thought, "this is really dumb.*

*I don't know what I feel. How am I supposed
to feel? I don't know how to feel. I can't feel"
I thought, "I don't understand. I must be
dreaming. I want to wake up. This can't be real."*

*I remember that sadness was the first feeling that I learned.
I saw it expressed on her face as my story I told.
Then my own feelings came as the tears, which had been held
so long, came gushing out like liquid black gold.*

*I remember in the beginning, the horrible
fear of my feelings, that caused nightmares.
This was all so new. I didn't know what
was coming up of which I had not been aware.*

*She gently and patiently kept telling me
that to heal I would need to feel the pain.
She assured me that I would not be alone.
She promised me that I would not go insane.*

*One by one as all the feelings came
up, the sadness, anger, grief, guilt and shame,
She kept reassuring me and reminding
me, that it wasn't my fault, I was not to blame.*

*Sometimes I experienced feelings
and I didn't know what they were called.
I would describe them to her and
she, with her wisdom, would name them all.*

I thought once that it would be helpful
if I'd received a manual with these feelings.
But, now that I think about it, it would
have taken away some of my joy from my healing.

It wasn't to long into this learning
and accepting of these beautiful gifts,
that I learned all the feelings that came
weren't of pain, as through them I would sift.

As I learned and grew spiritually by
accepting and depending on the God within,
I experienced feelings such as joy, peace,
comfort, and hope, where there had never been.

I've learned there are no "good" or "bad"
feelings, though some are painful and some are not.
They are all gifts of God that He gives to us
to learn more about Him as He works in our heart.

I recognize that I still have a lot to learn in
accepting and embracing these beautiful gifts from Him.
Just like the joy we receive from our children
when we've learned to unconditionally love and accept them.

Like anything precious, or of value, there are some rules or
responsibilities that come with the gift of feelings.
It's healthier if we learn to not numb, stuff, or deny them
because this would interfere with our process of healing.

At the same time, just like we don't tell all our business
and everything we know to everyone we happen to meet,
Though it's necessary to share our feelings, we must be careful
to choose a privileged few, not everyone on the street.

Learning about these feelings is a daily happening
for which God gives us abundant patience and Grace.
As long as we are living on this earth we will have
circumstances which brings feelings that we will have to face.

We have been taught that it's not the problems themselves that
teach, but the test is how we respond or react.
It's not the response to the problems, but to the feelings that
come with the problems, that we must keep in tact.

"So how do we do this?" you may be asking,
looking for a quick fix.
I don't have all the answers, but I know
in God's own time He'll teach us the tricks.

Hand Me Downs, Second Hand, and Borrowed

April 17, 1994

As a child, we learned by watching and mirroring
others that were our role models, usually our caretakers.
Little girls played dress up and let's pretend, while
little boys learned about the Dallas Cowboys and the Lakers.

As we grew into our own person and became adults, whether
we came from a dysfunctional family or not,
we learned about right and wrong, making choices, and
taking responsibility for our actions, even when things got hot.

Up until now our knowledge has been hand me downs, our
faith has been second hand and we learn our time here is a gift
we borrowed.

It's at this moment that we learn that we have nothing of our own. We don't know who we are, where we are going and our life is filled with sorrow.

We are then painfully thrown into a wild frenzy, frantically searching for some little grain of knowledge of our own, remembering about the God above, that we heard about and living with the guilt and shame for the wild seeds we have sown.

I believe that it's then, when we are ready, that God looks at us and smiles knowing we have been prepared to learn.
It's then, when we have come to our ropes end that we, with faith, can let go and let God teach us Himself and our life begins to turn.

It's because of His marvelous Grace and His eternal love for us that He takes the time to lovingly teach us step by step.
As long as we are willing to allow Him to work through us, He finds Joy in reminding us of His promises that He has kept.

No more do we have to be satisfied with "hand me down knowledge," for He graciously gives us His wisdom if we just ask.
No more do we have to live by "second hand faith" because He anxiously awaits to become our life and help us with each task.

Though the phenomenal gifts He blesses us with
along the way, are "borrowed" for a short time, it's okay.
That means they, just like His tender mercies and
His marvelous grace, are new and fresh with each new day.

One day we will leave this world as we know it to
live in a much better place, forever free of pain and sorrow.

One thing we will find there is that everything is brand new.
Nothing is "hand me downs, second hand, or borrowed."

God's Gift of Friendship

April 19, 1994

Because God can't set across the table
talking and listening to us over a cup of coffee,
He shares and loves through a friend,
which is a beautiful gift He gives to you and me.

It's through the arms of a friend that God
can reach out to embrace us with comfort and love.
It's through their ears, He can hear us. It's
through their mouth we can hear from Him above.

This world would indeed be a sad lonely
empty place if it were not for our special friends.
Their presence, their love and their
willingness is so unique, it's hard to know where to begin.

This kind of love is totally different than
what we feel for a child, parent or a spouse.
It's different than what we feel for a
sibling, a co-worker, roses, food, or our house.

Friends are another extraordinary workable
tool that God uses to help our spiritual part grow.
We are blest with the opportunity to learn
more about Him and us as the seeds of friendship, we sow.

Most of the time it's the warm bright
sunshine that He sends with our laughter,
that makes those seeds quickly
germinate and we see the results not long after.

Sometimes it may be through our shedding
tears from deep inside, He sends the gentle rain.
This allows those seeds to change and begin
to sprout while together, we work through our pain.

This friendship grows as we learn to
nurture first ourselves and then each other.
This makes the root system stronger and
our friendship can stand any kind of weather.

I would like to think this is
something that would last forever,
but because it is a borrowed gift, just
like life, sometimes the ties are severed.

It may be by death, miles or just His
timing, but sometimes we out grow each other.
It's then that God transplants us,
otherwise our roots may entangle and we smother.

This transplanting can be so very
painful as the one we love, we lose,
but it's a necessary part of our spiritual
growth as the strength within, we learn to use.

We carry some part of those we have been
privileged to know in this life, wherever we may go.
The part that is eternal, is the God within. This
is the part we share as seeds of new friendships we sow.

So when this marvelous gift is
offered you, don't hesitate to accept it,
knowing full well that it could last
a lifetime or only for a fleeting moment.

As we treat our precious friendship as the priceless
gift that it is, the length of time should be of no concern.
By accepting, giving, and being thankful for which we
are entrusted, our spirituality grows as God's love, we learn.

Is God Welcomed?

April 21, 1994

God does not abuse us, so we have no need to
fear him with the shaking in our boots kind of fear.
Tho He loves us and wants to guide us,
we must choose to let Him know we want Him near.

He is always a gentleman and will never force
Himself upon us. He waits to be invited to live within.
He waits patiently for us to welcome Him. He's
there watching as we mess up and have to start over again.

It's with innocent childlike faith and trust we believe
that He can change our life both internally and externally.
It's then that we can welcome Him to give us His
wisdom and knowledge and our spirituality grows eternally.

The angels in heaven and earth sing loud
Hosannas and the flood gates of joy spring open wide,
when we accept His abiding love as we welcome
Him as our new life and we become His eternal bride.

Daughter By Law

April 24, 1994

Though I wasn't privileged
to give you life,
you came to me by becoming
my son's wife.

I don't know that I could
love you any more,
If I had given birth to you myself
and that pain I bore.

I missed your growing up learning
to crawl and then walk,
but I get to watch you grow now
as I listen to you talk.

I'm glad my son was wise
enough to choose you.
It's one of the smartest thing
he ever chose to do.

I'm really thrilled you chose
my son and his family,
for I feel the one that has been
the most blest, is me.

Thank you for your love you give
to that special son of mine.
Thank you for being my daughter
by law so beautiful and kind.

You are a miraculous gift just because
you are an awesome creation of God.
I hope that you will always remember
this, as through this life you trod.

I love you, my daughter by law

Daughter By Birth

April 24, 1994

I remember the wonderment as I held you
in my arms for the first time so long ago.
I guess it's something a mother never
forgets as she watches her child grow.

I am so thankful that I not only was
allowed to give birth to you,
but to watch you grow from that
helpless tiny baby so new,

Into the beautiful caring loving
woman I see before me today,
so strong, secure, sure of yourself, as in
this world you make your own way.

Thank you for the wonderful joy
as well as the tiny bit of pain.
If I had it to all do over, you know
I would, because of all I've gained.

I'm so grateful to be your mom and
share with you this special place.
Tho you didn't get to choose me, nor I you,
I would, you know if that had been the case.

You are a miraculous gift just because
you are an awesome creation of God.
I hope that you will always remember
this, as through this life you trod.

I love you, my daughter

Son By Birth

April 24, 1994

You didn't choose me for your mom,
nor I you, for my son.
However, I think the match was good,
and I sure like the way it was done.

Watching you grow was certainly a
valuable learning experience.
I learned a little about independence,
acceptance, and of course patience.

It was certainly worth it all as I look
at the young man I know today.
You have become a responsible loving
caring person in so many ways.

I'm so thankful for the part of your life back
then and now that I get to share.

I'm thankful for all the things I see from you
toward others that show you care.

You are a miraculous gift just because
you are an awesome creation of God.
I hope that you will always remember
this, as through this life you trod.

I love you, my son

Son By Law

April 26, 1994

You hold a special place of your own
in my heart, because you
have been entrusted with a gift
that I was entrusted with too.

Years ago she came to me as
my beautiful baby girl.
That was the day God smiled and gave
me more wealth than pearls.

She grew up and became a beautiful
woman in her own right.
She fell in love with you and
chose to become you wife.

You've accepted the awesome responsibility
for this priceless gift in your care,
yet you've allowed her to still be her own
unique person, which now adays is rare.

This truly makes you a son by law
in my sight and I'm pleased
that you, with wisdom, chose each other
and that moment you seized.

I love you and trust you with
this special gift of mine.
May God bless you both in a special way
as together you march through time.

You are a miraculous gift just because
you are an awesome creation of God.
I hope that you will always remember
this, as through this life you trod.

I love you, my son by law

Real Love

May 4, 1994

I ask God the other day to teach me
about the mystery of real love,
the kind that was patient that would last
and came from Him above.
"My love is a paradox," He said, "the more
you give away, the more it grows.
Love does not smother, posses, or chain one to another.
It freely and gently comes and goes.

How important is love?" He asked
with compassion in His eyes.

"If an infant doesn't get it in the beginning,
it eventually gives up and dies.

Falling in love is really not a choice, it's
effortless and just a happening.
Real love can grow from it or the relationship
ends or becomes like a trapping.

Real love is a choice. We choose if we want it
and if we want to keep it alive.
It takes courage, attention, commitment, and
willingness to work, to survive.

Real love is selfish, yet unselfish, just
look at the reason for Jesus' birth.
I wanted more sons, so I sent Him to live
and dwell in each of you while on earth.

When you truly extend and give of yourself
this helps others to know
that you love them. This is nurturing and
beneficial as their spiritual part grows.

As this is done, you will become aware that
your spiritual part is growing too.
Again, remember, the more you give away,
the more that comes back to you.

Love is a mystery, but it's really not. It's just
the willingness to give of yourself,
to nurture the spiritual growth of not just
another but of ones own self.

You must first have this love for yourself before
you can give it to another so freely.
For how can you give away something which you do
not possess, but which you are so needy?

It's the knowledge that you, with your imperfections, are a
unique creation of mine that gives you this authority.
You are a beautiful child of the King of Kings.
Through your veins flows the blood of royalty.

Real love is not a feeling, tho there are feelings of love.
Real love is giving and not expecting anything in return.
Real love is safe and doesn't, in any way, hurt another.
Real love is a gift, of which wisdom, you have learned."

God is in the Storms

May 5, 1994

I'm reminded of the overwhelming
power and energy in the storms that ascends.
There is such a sense of helplessness
and being out of control as we watch the winds.

I hear it in the thunder so loud and rumbling.
I see it in the lightening which lights up the sky.
I see it in the floods that can wash things away.
I see it in winds that break buildings and people die.

I guess if there was a time
for healthy fear, well, here it is.
It's during this time I feel so
small, so minute in this plan of His.

In the devastation of it all, we may forget
that the same power that we see in the storm,
can be used to help us get through the rough
and tough times and brings us back to the norm.

It's also at this frightful time I
marvel at His power and am reminded
that He is just as powerful in the
storms of life which may leave us blinded.

Blinded to His wisdom, awesomeness,
goodness, and love for us along the way.
We forget that after the storms we have the
rainbow, reminding us that He's with us to stay.

Warning, Warning, Warning

May 5, 1994

We need to take shelter because we are
in a severe storm alert until we die.
Some could be severe. Need to prepare.
There's no time to watch the sky.

We need to have knowledge as to what
we are to do to prepare.
God delights in giving us His Wisdom
as we go to Him in prayer.

He gives us warnings and expects us to pass
them along to those who are near,
as we help each other to find peace and safety
in His sheltering arms so secure.

Times when it is really rough, we may just
have to hang on and ride it out.
We know that the storm won't last forever
and He is with us, without a doubt.

If the storm leaves damage, we can look at the ruins,
cry, ask why, and wring our hands in despair,
or we can, with the help of others, start to clean up
rebuild, and be thankful that our life was spared.

Victim, Survivor, and Thriver

May 5, 1994

I remember being the victim, so helpless,
hopeless, wounded, and all alone.
I remember the fear, the knowing and the not knowing,
the pain of being in my own "twilight zone."

Through His matchless amazing Grace, He gave me
the courage to commit to this Recovery Journey.
At the time, not knowing what was ahead, I set out
with His faith to find this lost person, "ME."

As each painful memory, and each
painful feeling emerged,
as each dark secret I revealed, I felt more
strength as my past I purged.

It was then that I learned that I was no longer
a victim. Those times were over.
It was then, that I was made aware, that through the
Grace of God I had become a Survivor.

As I learned to feel, as I was guided, as I was taught to search
and the more I worked to change, I became stronger.
It was when I accepted that I was powerless over what
happened, and its effects, that I learned I wasn't alone any longer.

I had the authority to give it all to my Higher Power and
through His Grace learn as He gave me wisdom.
I found the more I asked, the more He gave, the more
I depended on Him the bigger He would become.

Somewhere in the midst of all this, I noticed that the every
day circumstances weren't as painful or as overwhelming.
I became aware that tho there was still pain and suffering,
there was also an abundance of joy and peace, that kept coming.

It was then that I recognized that I had left the powerless
victim role to become that joyful hopeful strong survivor.
But, just like God, He didn't stop there. He gave me much
more than I could have asked by blessing me as a "Thriver."

I'm in Love

May 7, 1994

There's a bounce in my walk
and a spring in my step.
There's joy in my heart and a
song on my lips.

There's a new twinkle
in my eye.
There's a long never
ending sigh.

There's compassion and love
for everyone around.
There's an appreciation
for every little sound.

The grass is greener and
the trees are taller.
Life's little problems
all seem smaller.

The birds seem to sing
prettier and fly lower.
Yet at times, like my heart,
they seem to soar.

Everything around seems more
vivid and brighter.
The weight of the world on my
shoulder seems lighter.

I have such gratitude for God's
majestic beautiful landscapes.
I'm thankful for the times in a
good book, I can quietly escape.

There's a fullness in my heart
that I just can't explain.
There's joy and peace even in the
midst of suffering and pain.

I look for an explanation for all this
excitement, wonderment and hype.
All I can come up with is that I have fallen
head over heels in love with life.

In the Stillness of the Early Morning

May 8, 1994

In the stillness of the early morning,
God and I take our walk.
In the stillness of the early morning,
is when we can quietly talk.

It's at this time there are no phones
ringing, or any other interruptions.
It's at this time I can thank Him for His
goodness and ask for my daily instructions.

It's in the stillness of the morning everything is quiet as
we are all waking up from a good night's rest.
In the stillness of the early morning, it seems that the
air smells fresher and the birds sing their best.

It's like the new morning brings with it newness of
spirit, a new hope, and a brand new start.
I can make it what ever kind of day I choose because
it begins in my thoughts and in my heart.

I look forward with anticipation to our
early morning times together.
I have more energy from within and my
health has never been better.

During this, our special private time together, I'm
walking so my heart will beat longer,
and at the same time these enlightening talks help
my spiritual part grow and become stronger.

In the stillness of the early morning,
God and I take our walk.
In the stillness of the early morning,
is when we can quietly talk.

Teach Me

May 9, 1994

My prayer, Father, is that you will teach
me to love as you have loved me.
Teach me how to give this love as you've
given so abundantly and free.

Teach me, Father, how to receive
love from others that give.
Teach me to never take their love for
granted as long as I live.

Teach me, Father, how to love not only those who
are lovable, but those that are unlovable.
Remind me Father that they are your children, too
and therefore are loved and forgivable.

Teach me forgiveness, Father, as you
have forgiven me so many times.
Teach me how to forgive not only for their
sakes, but for this healing of mine.

Remind me, Father, in your most
gentle special patient way
of the forgiveness you show each of
us through your mercy every day.

Teach me, Father, about the paradox
of life with all its confusing contrasts.
Help me to understand the differences
between the temporal and that which lasts.

Remind me, Father, of the futility of instant
gratification and immediate pleasure.
Yet teach me the importance of living for today,
not in the past or for tomorrow's treasures.

Teach me, Father, about living, loving and
doing for today as if it were my last.
Teach me, Father, to start the day by meeting
with you first because before I know it the day is past.

Teach me, Father, as the day to swiftly
comes to an end and the night comes,
with Thanksgiving and gratefulness in my
heart give you praise for a job well done.

As I Have Received, I Freely Give

May 10, 1994

Through others, I have felt your love.
Through others, I have felt your embrace.
Through others, I have felt your acceptance.
Through others, I have felt your comfort.

Through others, I have felt your forgiveness.
Through others, I have felt your tenderness.
Through others, I have felt your gentleness.
Through others, I have felt your kindness.

Through others, I have felt your warmth.
Through others, I have felt your compassion.
Through others, I have felt your strength.
Through others, I have felt your encouragement.

To others, let me give your love.
To others, let me give your embrace.
To others, let me give your acceptance.
To others, let me give your comfort.

To others, let me give your forgiveness.
To others, let me give your tenderness.
To others, let me give your gentleness.
To others, let me give your kindness.

To others, let me give your warmth.
To others, let me give your compassion.
To others, let me give your strength.
To others, let me give your encouragement.

Memories

May 10, 1994

Beautiful memories are a pleasant most welcomed
visit from the ones we love when we are apart.
When they, for what ever reason, can't be with us,
God sends them through our minds and hearts.

Memories are another awesome gift that God,
in His Grace, sends to bless along the way.
With our precious memories we can visit and carry
with us those we love through out the day.

All memories are not beautiful or fill us with joy.
Some are down right ugly and fill us with fear.
The painful memories are a standing invitation
from our Heavenly Father who is always near.

An invitation to accept the pain as the gift intended
and then for our spiritual growth, give it all to Him.
He's the only one that can take those painful memories
and make something wondrously beautiful from them.

It's important for us to remember, as we journey day in
and day out, that memories we are always making.
It's the choices we make, with the knowledge we have, that
determines the kind of memories with us we will be taking.

I Love the Spring

May 19, 1994

I love the Spring time, it's my favorite.
I just love the newness of everything.
I love the trees budding with new leaves.
I love the fragrant clean smells of Spring.

I love crocus peeking through the soil telling
us warm weather will be here pretty soon.
They are such brave little flowers being the
first, then the daffodils and iris start to bloom.

I love the warm sun shinny days filled with
energy and the cool clear starry nights.
I love the little squirrels scampering around
and the laughing children flying their kites.

I love the warm gentle rains that come
with their beautiful clouds of blue gray.
I love to hear the baby birds start to sing
as their parents send them on their way.

I love Spring because it reminds me of
new beginnings, new starts, and change.
It reminds me that nothing has or can stay
the same. Everything is within our range.

God did an excellent job when He made the Spring.
He painted beautiful landscapes far and wide.
He painted beautiful sunsets and sunrises, but none
compare with the beauty He does on us inside.

He has a way of putting Spring within each of us.
With that comes our energy and our newness.
With it comes the gentle rains of tears along with
the laughter, the joy and mountains of happiness.

She Wears Her Scars Well

May 22, 1994

She was a cute free spirited energetic
helpful little girl of three
when she reached up that day and
grabbed the container of hot tea.

In just a moment, in not seeing,
before she could be stopped,
it had spilled on her and she
screamed because it was so hot.

Second and third degree burns
on her little neck and shoulders
pained her terribly then and
continued even as she got older.

Though the traumatic event itself
left scars on the outside,
it unnoticeably had left scars within,
that she tried to hide.

On many shopping trips to buy cute
fun clothes, she felt limited
because it was either sleeveless or
tank tops that she rejected.

She felt embarrassed, and self conscience
because the kids were so cruel.
Their teasing and laughing made it really
hard when she went to school.

She covered them up the best she knew how,
not wanting others to have to see.
She didn't want them looking and feeling bad
for themselves or offering sympathy.

As long as she carefully kept them covered, they
were her secrets and no one had to know.
She just couldn't let anyone get close to her because
then her scars she would have to show.

Deep inside she felt she was not normal, why would
anyone love her and her ugly scars.
She was not aware that the effects from the burns had
come to out weigh the burns themselves by far.

She was a perfect lovable daughter, sister and friend
always looking out for others needs.
Her own needs she pushed aside as others she tried
so hard to care for and to please.

She ran to God because He promised to love and accept
her the way she was even with her scars and sins.
If she could just go to Bible study several times a week
and be religious she knew she could make amends.

She knew with God she could become
lovable and thus forgiven
as she worked so hard to become an
overcomer and go to heaven.

In her relationships along the way with
the religious young men
she was the self sacrificing woman who
knew her place, again.

After awhile, knowing she was ready, her loving Father
stepped in after seeing her in her confusion and pain.
He, through His grace, had a new happy growth experience
for her that would leave her life not ever the same.

She met and fell in love with a wonderful cowboy
who she married after becoming his friend.
She has learned to love and accept herself for the
inner beauty and strength of the God within.

She knows that though the scars are still there,
it's the beauty within that everyone sees.
She wears her scars very well, this daughter of
mine who has always been a joy to me.

I Wear My Scars Well

May 22, 1994

I was a cute, timid lonely
little girl of three or four
when the abuse started and
became more and more.

It wasn't just one perpetrator and it wasn't just
once that parts of my childhood was lost.
Though that's all it took for the harm to be done
as my needs for love were met at a high cost.

Year after year while growing up, feelings were
being numbed as my pain I had to hide.
Year after year the feelings of guilt and shame were
pushed down deeper and deeper inside.

Though the traumatic event itself was over in a flash,
the long standing effects would be with me as I grew.
I had to wear a false mask pretending everything was
fine because I had to make sure that no one ever knew.

I felt embarrassed and self conscience at the thought
of someone finding out, because of my shame.
I knew it must have been my fault and that I had
to accept all the horrible guilt and blame.

I covered it up the best I knew how,
not wanting others to see.
Guess if they knew, just like I did,
they would have to blame me.

As long as I carefully kept them covered, they
were my secrets and no one had to know.
That meant I couldn't let anyone get close to me because
I might forget and my inner pain I would show.

Deep inside I felt I was not normal and no one
would love me if the secrets they knew about.
I was not aware that later the effects from the abuse
would be what would bring the secrets out.

I grew up trying to be the perfect daughter and then later the
perfect wife and mother, taking care of everyone else's needs.
My own needs I denied, stuffed and pushed aside as all
the others I tried so hard to take care of and to please.

As a child, I had given my heart to God and
ask for His forgiveness from all my sins.
But because of the continuing abuse and since
it was my fault, I felt unworthy to ask Him again.

I couldn't ask God for His love that I so desperately needed
so I had to find it from others that were not safe.
More of the effects of the abuse left me feeling so dirty and
so bad as each time afterward the shame, I had to face.

Once again I was told to repent of my sins and just like
the prodigal son, God would forgive me once more.
I found a place to lay down my life for Him and outwardly
find the happiness that I had not known before.

When that opportunity was taken from me and again I was
left on my own with no place to serve the Almighty God,
I didn't know how to keep working for Him to assure my
salvation was still there and escape His chastening rod.

After a while, knowing I was ready, my loving Father stepped
in after seeing me in all my confusion and pain.
He, through His grace, had a new spiritual growth experience
for me that would leave my life not ever the same.

With His strength and His courage, I learned to put one foot
in fount of the other as this healing journey we started.
The more pain I experienced, the more grace He so freely gave
and I know He's living through me and we'll never be parted.

I know the more I recognize that I don't have to handle life's
sufferings alone, the more I give it over to Him to bear,
the bigger He grows within me and the more joy and peace
I have with others to lovingly and gratefully share.

I know that the scars from my past will always be there, to
remind me not only of the awful pain, but of His Grace that
He has shown.
I will wear my scars well because God has made from them
something beautiful from within as His beauty and love I so
willingly make known.

Courage

May 22, 1994

Courage is not in fear's place.
Courage is not the opposite of fear.

Courage can only be there in fear's face.
Courage can only be there when fear is near.

We can have fear without courage,
but we can't have courage without fear.

Fear, we don't have to ask for,
but courage is not so readily there.

Fear keeps us bound and stuck,
but courage makes the way clear.

Fear can make us sad and alone,
but courage can give us a smile to wear.

Fear is a gift to warn us of danger,
but courage is a gift to hold dear.

The Door to My Past

May 24, 1994

I thought when I closed it the last time
that I had said good bye to the past.
I thought finally I had found peace,
joy, and hope that would last.

I thought I had said good bye to that part
of my life with it's loneliness and pain.
I thought, "now I can get on with my wonderful
new life and all that I have to gain."

I felt so grown up with all this knowledge
of my new spiritual growth and learning.
Finally, I could relax because now I had the
tools to keep my wonderful world turning.

I had learned that I couldn't change the past
with its unmerciful pain and sorrow,
but I had God and I knew He would give me
the needed strength to face tomorrow.

It wasn't the circumstances of today that had
to be faced, for that would be a steal.
I could face it all, now that I knew that it was
my feelings with which I had to deal.

Then it happened while I was on my merry way
basking in the Spring sunshine.
It happened with no warning. I had not expected
a thing. It was just God's time.

The door to my past just blew open and painfully
drew me back through it again.
I quickly forgot everything that I had learned about
feelings and circumstances as I ran.

Without knowing it I ran to the familiar, I didn't
want to. It hurt so bad, but I couldn't stop.
The feelings of loneliness, rejection, hopelessness
and abandonment nearly sent me over the top.

It was there to haunt me once more. I wanted to run
away. I didn't want to face it. I just wanted to die.
I was so angry, but I didn't know with whom. I guess
at everyone, even God and then I started to cry.

From deep within, the pain of my "little girl" once more,
had to be recognized and she had to be held and loved.
I was reminded that it wasn't just my pain that I had to
bear, but all of hers that she so long had shoved.

That's why the past has to be revisited. That's why the
door to my past can't remain closed forever.
Something may happen today that triggers those same
feelings that she so creatively learned to cover.

I know now that it's okay to feel those helpless feelings
and ask for someone to listen and hold me.
It's okay not to be the adult all the time, and to need
nurturing, attention, and help for the past to see.

In a safe place, with a safe person we were
allowed to scream to talk and to feel.
The anger came up, the hurt came out and
as she listened, we were able to heal.

It came and went just about as quick
as a warm gentle Spring rain.
Before I knew it, the door was closed
again and gone was the pain.

My Grief

May 30, 1994

I liken the pain of my grief to laying on a table
and someone comes in with a knife
and with no anesthetic, cuts my chest wide open.

Not saying a word, with both hands they reach deep inside
disconnecting my heart from the vessels and the tissues
that had held it so secure and safe all these years.

I watch them as they, not aware or caring about my pain,
take my still beating bleeding heart and gently
lay it on a cold shiny table across the room.

As I watch them, I wonder, "why am I paralyzed?
Why can't I stop them? Why can't I speak?
Why can't I scream and tell them this hurts?"

From where I am laying, all alone in a pool of my blood,
with my chest open wide, I can still see it beating, across
the room, as I'm wondering how could I still be alive.

Then I wonder, "am I still alive? I see my heart beating
so I must be. Somewhere once I remember hearing that
as long as my heart was beating I was alive."

But as I look at myself bleeding and I'm feeling much colder now
as the life force drains from me, I think, "but this can not be, for
I'm losing blood. I have no heart inside of me. Am I dead?"

Then I wonder, "was I ever alive? Was I ever a being?
Where did I come from? Where am I going?
What was I? What am I now?"

I'm someone who lost something that I never had. I'm
someone feeling the pain of my grief. I feel like someone just
cut my heart out and I can see it beating from across the room.....

It Takes Courage

June 1, 1994

It takes courage to be yourself, to take off the
mask you've worn so long and be real.
It takes courage to risk rejection from the
ones you love by saying what you feel.

It takes courage to listen to the quiet
gentle voice inside and obey.
It takes courage to believe in yourself
and say what you have to say.

It takes courage to want to face
it head on and accept the pain.
It takes courage especially when you
alone know what you have to gain.

It takes courage when those you trust
don't seem to understand why.
It takes courage to face the pain instead
of just numbing or wanting to die.

It takes courage when it's you alone that
knows what has to be done to be set free.
It takes courage to do it all alone because
those around for some reason just can't see.

It takes courage to recognize what you need
or want as you journey from day to day.
It take courage to admit that you have needs or
wants and then to ask for help along the way.

It takes courage to say that you must do
this today for the past you want to heal.
It takes courage to accept it, to talk about it,
to grieve and to cry as the feelings you feel.

It takes courage but there is an over abundant
supply that's free, just for the asking.
It takes courage, but when the choice is made,
it's His peace and serenity you'll be accepting.

Spinning Plates

June 8, 1994

Life seems to be comprised of spinning
plates on a pole one after the other.
You get one started and another pops
up then another and then another.

Before you know it, it's a mad rush running
here and there to keep them spinning.
You can't slow down, you can't rest, you certainly
can't stop or you won't be winning.

About the time you think you are getting comfortable,
you notice from nowhere another appears.
Another glance and you see one way at the other end
start to wobble and it brings up fears.

As you're rushing over to it, you see it held there
slowly spinning on its own by another power.
You're so engrossed in this phenomenal thing you forget
about the others, maybe for seconds or hours.

When you jar yourself awake and in terror
you glance around expecting the worse,
You see each plate is still slowly spinning,
reminding you of the God of the universe.

Baby Sarah

July 3, 1994

Forever it seems, we patiently
waited for you.
A precious baby girl named Sarah
all brand new.

We shopped, painted, sewed, and
fixed your room.
Then sat back and waited knowing
you'd be here soon.

As you were kept so safe, warm and
secure in your mother's womb,
Love for you was already growing in our
hearts as God was making room.

You were loved before you made your
dramatic grand entrance.
All of a sudden we had to have faith and a
different kind of patience.

I prayerfully watched through the nursery window
as the nurse held your limp little arms.
I begged, through tears, that God would not take
you away. I felt peace and I felt no alarm.

For a few minutes, though it seemed
forever, you gave us quite a scare.
But God, in His Grace and mercy gave the
doctors wisdom and you are here.

As I hold you close to me, I know I'll
never take you for granted.
You are indeed a precious little miracle,
just the way God planned it.

My faith and love for God is even
stronger because of you.
I know as you grow up, He'll teach
you all about this, too.

Love, Nanny

My Freedom

July 4, 1994

I have lived and survived the painful
lonely part of my past.
I have grieved the losses and am daily
learning to accept them at last.

As I became aware of the debilitating
self defeating effects,
That had left me with recognizable scars
and emotional defects,

I learned I didn't have to live as a weak victim.
I could learn to grow and be stronger.

I learned that I had the power to change that
part of me that I didn't need any longer.

I know that the celebration of Independence Day
means different things to each one of us.
Today, to me, it means freedom to choose to accept
the past instead of existing forever grievous.

Today I choose not only to accept and embrace
this part of me, but also to be thankful.
Because of it, I learned to depend on the God within
who is all knowing and so powerful.

The reality is that everything that has happened up to now has
molded and shaped me into my own uniqueness.
Though I have imperfections and make mistakes, I have a
deep love for myself mixed with confidence, and acceptance.

It's because of the good and the bad of my past I became the
strong, courageous, sensitive, caring person that I am today.
It's because of the Power and Grace of God that I can, with
peace in my heart, hold my head up high and with joy,
truthfully say,

"I have lived and survived the painful
lonely part of my past.
I have grieved the losses and can now,
with freedom, live at last."

This is my freedom.

How Do I Say Good-bye?

June 11-August 3, 1994

It would be easier if you were a friend moving
away to another town or another state.
We would hug, promise to keep in touch by phone
or mail and to visit, thus accepting our fate.

If we were going through the loss of getting a divorce,
pulling up roots, and blaming each other,
the loss would still be painful as we relived the good times
and the memories of promising to stay together.

If you were terminally ill with not much longer to live, I might
could learn to accept the idea of losing you and not seeing you
again.
We would enjoy every moment we had and fill it with extra
love and care as we watch time pass like an hour glass full of
sand.

If your death was sudden and I didn't have the chance to say
good-bye and once more say the words," I love you,"
I would grieve, be depressed, and miss you along with all that
we could have shared, but that's what I would be expected to
do.

I would understand all this. I would learn to accept it as a
painful loss I would remember that losses are the price we pay
for living.
I would learn that I had to go on with my life. All the love I
had received from you and had for you, to others I would
keep on giving.

This relationship is different. You aren't a friend moving away. You aren't someone I've lived with that I'm divorcing. You're not a loved one that I'm having to lose to death, or an accident. You're a vessel used by God and our time together is ending.

Then comes phrases like, "letting go, moving along, dealing with the pain while grieving the loss" and the real big one is "saying good-bye."
This is hard to do when this lesson was not taught. Instead, those I loved were snatched away or disappeared leaving me wanting to die.

Our client/therapist relationship is over. I don't need you to help me with my challenges any longer so there's no reason to continue to write or call.
We can't be friends, go out for coffee or just chat. I hear it's for our protection, this "ethics" thing, which I don't understand much at all.

At first I wondered if it was just a cop out that therapists used when they couldn't be truthful and look you in the eye.
I wondered if it was that they didn't want a friendship with a needy dependent former client, so someone made up the lie.

My feelings of love and the spiritual bond that God has blest us with has not changed, they are still the same.
It's confusing because when I love someone, I see us able to share, laugh and cry together, as our friendship we claim.

You taught me to follow my instincts as I learn to listen to the quiet little voice inside.
Because of the eternal bond of love I felt, I offered you my friendship, which had to be denied.

As I turned this all over to my Higher Power and asked
for His Wisdom as to know what to do,
I was reminded that it was His love that I wanted to
give and it was His love I had received from you.

God gave me a beautiful life. With it came innocence, trust,
the capacity to love and to receive love and most of all, hope.
With it came basic needs and the right to ask for help to get
those needs met as I would learn about living and how to
cope.

He gave me the right to learn to love myself, to grow up
feeling safe, secure, unconditionally loved and accepted.
All that was taken from me over and over again as I lost the
ones I loved and was abused by the other caretakers that I
trusted.

God then brought you into my life years later, to teach me
how to find His knowledge as I found for myself what I didn't
get to learn.
He worked through you to restore my hope as you guided me.
I felt the unconditional love and acceptance and my life
started to turn.

I feel that God, working through you, gave me the
opportunity to learn how to reclaim and replace some of what
I lost.
It hasn't been easy and it's taken a lot of hard work and
courage just to face the grief and pain, but it's been worth the
cost.

Is it any wonder that with you allowing God to work through
you, I have found a new life that's so much healthier?

Is it any wonder that with this bond, I want to share with you a small part of this new life, making us spiritually wealthier?

I grieve because I no longer have the right to share with you the great "God Deals" He continues to send my way.
It's this part of my life, for your hope, encouragement and growth, that I want to give back to you to bless you each day.

This is not because I need someone to share these things with for God has blest me abundantly with loving family and friends.
I feel, that like me, you haven't stopped loving, caring and rejoicing with me tho our client/therapist relationship had to end.
I grieve because I'll always wonder what could have been or what might have been, but there's no way to know.
So, again the questions keep coming to mind, how do I learn to say good bye to what we didn't have and how do I let it go?

I kept asking you over and over, " but what do I do with these feelings of affection that I have for you?"
Over and over again you would give me the same answer, " it's your choice. You'll know what to do."

As of late, I have been learning about the awesome gift of acceptance. It started with the acceptance of the good and bad of my past.
With this came the freedom to accept and love me as myself because now I know this is truly the only love for me that will last.
I'm wondering if I might not use this gift of acceptance and take the risk to choose to accept this bond of affection as a priceless gift.

With the acceptance of this unique gift comes the freedom to choose to keep it all to myself or to choose to share and someone else's heart to lift.

I accept that now is not the appropriate time to share with you anything more of the feelings I will gratefully carry in my heart. I'm thankful and celebrate the time we've had, the lessons we've learned, the joy of our growth, and I accept, we have to be apart.

I'll take one day at a time as each new challenge I face. I'll be patient, gentle and kind with myself as I accept, mixed with the joy, life's pain.
I'll live each day to the fullest as I work and play. To others I will share my God given gifts of experiences, courage, love, and hope, of what I gain.

Another New Beginning

August 4, 1994

The sun rises high in the Eastern sky
and a new day is beginning.
With each new day that dawns, a new start
and a new hope it is bringing.

As I watch the beautiful orange sun sinking slowly in
the Western sky, another day is ending.
I can rejoice in my accomplishments while I learn and
grow from the mistakes that I'm regretting.

With calm assurance of my Father's love in my
heart, I welcome this day's closing.

As the blackness of night falls around me, because
of my faith, I feel no fear imposing.

A time of complete rest is given to me as my mind,
body and soul needs continual renewing.
I trust and believe that with each sun going down,
I will soon welcome another one appearing.

As the sun comes up and the new day starts, yesterday's
successes and failures I start forgetting.
The newness of light brings with it new choices and new
challenges along with another new beginning.

I Believe in Miracles

August 10, 1994

When I see the colors of a new sunrise
playing across the skies,
When I feel the words of a new poem
from within me start to rise,

When I touch the soft hair and tiny fingers
of my granddaughter so small,
When I've taken care of myself, believed in
myself, and I feel ten feet tall,

When I smell the fragrant essence
of a dew kissed flower,
When I make it through a rough day
not on mine, but God's power,

When I taste the tart sweetness of
fuzzy juicy cold peaches,
When I'm still enough to listen to the God
within as He patiently teaches,

When I hear the melodious happy
laughter of children at play,
When I can close my eyes in rest thanking
God for another growth day,

When I feel such joy for the little gifts I've received
in life that before I've taken for granted,
When I learn something new from the experiences
within my life He's so beautifully painted.

These are but a few of the many reasons I believe in
the miracles that God delights in sending.
Because He's our Father and we're His beloved children,
He rejoices as we accept the gifts He keeps on giving.

I'm Missing Her Again, God

August 18, 1994

I'm missing her again, God. Over four months ago
we courageously said our good byes.
There with her, feeling such love and gratitude,
neither one of us left with dry eyes.

I'm so thankful, God, for these memories. I'm
thankful for the wisdom she shared.
I'm thankful You blest both of us. I'm thankful
for the ways she showed she cared.

I'm missing her again, God. I miss her comforting words
and her gentle voice with the soft accent.
I miss the love and concern in her eyes. I miss watching
you work through her during the hours spent.

I'm missing her again, God. I miss the waiting with
exciting anticipation for our next learning session.
A time she listened and heard. A time I would accept the
challenges and eagerly work to learn the lesson.

I'm missing her again, God, but for some miraculous
reason, it feels amazingly different this time.
As I replay the words of wisdom she shared, I feel
my eyes are open and I'm no longer blind.

Thank you, God, for this unexpected visit with her. In my mind
I can see her sitting in her chair with her coffee, pen, and pad.
Like a student who loves to learn from a teacher who loves to
teach, I miss her, God, but this time I'm only a tiny bit sad.

Mandy, My Niece

September 6, 1994

I wish for you, Mandy my love,
special miracles from our Father above.

I wish for you my Mandy, safety and health
for this is something more precious than wealth.

I wish for you, Mandy my sweet,
happy dreams while you quietly sleep.

I wish for you my playful Mandy Pandy,
more sweetness of life than a pocket full of candy.

I wish for you my Mandy, a heart forever young
and I wish for you more songs of joy to be sung.

I wish for you my Mandy, joy and peace from within
that comes with knowledge learned from where you've been.

I'm so thankful my beautiful precious Mandy girl,
for God's gift of our love which is more priceless than pearls.

I'll always be thankful my gentle loving Mandy so kind,
for your love and laughter helps heal my body, soul, and mind.

I'm forever thankful for the knowledge, Mandy my dear,
that in our hearts and in our thoughts we'll always be near.

Teach Me to Listen

September 30, 1994

God, I'm really having trouble hearing
you. Can't you please speak a little louder?
There is so much static bouncing around
in my head. I can't hear you above the clatter.

I know there are times when I'm not so busy,
without question, you come through clear as a bell.
Yet, at times in the daily rat race as I'm running
here and there, it seems that I can't hear you very well.

Sometimes the reception is not good because
there's so much noise and confusion going on in my head.
I have so many doubts and fears because I'm not sure
which voice is yours and I'm not sure about what's being said.

I know it would really help if you could
try to speak a little louder, God and not whisper?
Sometimes I can't hear what you are saying.
You seem so far away, could you come a little closer?

How can I follow your direction
if you don't talk loud enough for me to hear?
How can I hear you if you stay
so far away? Won't you please come near?

God, can't you speak a little
louder please or maybe you could repeat?
If I'm to make choices, I need to
hear what they are before I can take that leap.

What, God? You're telling me
to close my mouth, be quiet and listen?
But God, I need you to know
that I can't hear you. Is it the distance?

What, God? You say you are
always close? You are always near?
If it's not the distance that is the
problem, what makes me unable to hear?

But, God, I don't understand what is it
then? What's keeping me from hearing your voice?
It's what, God? You say that I've not
been listening? You say this has been my choice?

You say you are here with me
every moment to help guide me through the day?
Every decision I have to make you
give of your wisdom to teach me along the way?

However, if I'm trying to listen to what's
going on around me, instead of your quiet voice,
then that's what gets me into trouble and
I make mistakes, but again, that was my choice?

With all my heart, God, I want to
learn to listen to your voice. Can you teach me how?
If I will be still and if I'm quiet, can
you hurry and start teaching me this lesson now?

You say if it starts to get really
noisy in my head from all the other things,
then I can listen in my heart, the
place you dwell and from where your love springs?

For it's there the wisdom which
I've found through the knowledge I gain,
can be graciously drawn from to
teach me through my mistakes and pain?

So, my prayer from now on, as I spend
time with you at the beginning of each new day,
is not just to lead, guide and direct me, but
to remind me to be quiet so I can hear what you say.

Wow!!! It's amazing, God what happens when I choose
to stop yelling, screaming, kicking, and fighting your system.
It's really quite simple. All I have to do is be still, be
quiet, and reverent as I listen from within for your wisdom.

Where Did the Pain Go?

October 7, 1994

Where did it go? When did it leave me, this
horrible excruciating tormenting pain from my past?
I thought this was something that would always be with me.
It would forever be a heavy cloud over me cast.

This is a loss that I joyfully praise God for.
It's a loss that brings tears of gladness instead of grief.
The cloud of sadness is no longer surrounding me.
Instead, through the knowledge of God, I've found relief.

The wounds of the past were forever being
reopened and the healing could never be completed.
They were grossly infected and unclean because
all these years they had gone uncared for and untreated.

Even before I was aware of the wounds and that
there was healing that needed to be done, God knew.
He brought me to a place that I realized my pain
was to big for me to handle and I didn't know what to do.

As I admitted to Him that I, in my ignorance,
could not survive this life changing task without His help,
He graciously and patiently gave me His gift of
knowledge by working through others as well as my self.

He placed in my life and worked through gifted therapists
who I believe became my Recovery Angels for this journey.
He gave hope and encouragement through the wisdom of
good friends, supporters, and family. He lovingly did all this
for me.

Through the validating experiences of others who shared their
inspiration through their books, I found a healing balm.
God blest me with knowledge through the gift of my poetry,
which reminds me of the way He taught King David through
his Psalms.

Are the wounds completely healed now? Is my healing on the
surface or does it go deep inside to the core?
So where did my pain from the past go? When did it leave
me? Will it ever come back to hurt me any more?

I am steadfast in my knowledge, as I observe with awe this
beautiful healthier person that I am blest to be today,
that because I learned, one day at a time to accept this pain
and learn from it, through God's healing it has been taken away.

As for the wounds, they are completely changed. Except for
tiny pink scars you would never know they were there.
With the healing ointment of God's love we have worked
together to clean and medicate each one as we became aware.

The tiny pink scars will be with me only as gentle reminders,
not of just the pain alone,
but of the phenomenal, awesome healing grace and love that
my Heavenly Father has shown.

From the experience of this pain, which has been a wonderful
teacher, I continue daily to spiritually learn and grow.
Lessons in love, acceptance, courage, and responsibility are
enriched by the discovery of this person I've always been, but
didn't know.

Because of the wisdom I have within me, I know I can
face, endure, learn, and grow from any mistakes or pain that

comes my way.
Where does all this faith and confidence come from? It comes from the knowledge of the faith and confidence giver, who gives every day.

My Wounds Are Healed

October 8, 1994

For years these ugly wounds
had existed open, unclean and infected.
The debilitating poison flowing
through my body, soul, and mind undetected.

For years this poison continually
contaminated my body, soul, and mind,
until one day by the grace of God,
I saw these wounds to which I had been blind.

As the years of numbing stopped working
and the horrible pain began to surface more each day,
I soon learned that these wounds could no
longer be taken care of by just covering with bandaids.

It was only then I became aware
of the choice to begin this healing journey.
It was only then that I learned
it was my task and it had to begin with me.

I wasn't long into this healing journey that I
learned the therapist, supporters and friends were not enough.
I chose to seek the help and knowledge from my Higher
Power because parts of this recovery had become really rough.

Through insight and knowledge, I
learned that God, with my precious tears of grief,
properly cleansed each wound one by
one which began the treatment to bring some relief.

The cleansing was indeed painful
and caused a lot of changes to have to be made.
I know now, as I experience joy and peace,
that it was worth it all, this price that had to be paid.

The hardest part of my recovery was to take
the first step and I had to do it. No one could do it for me.
It was then that I became aware that I would
not be alone as I was healing on this recovery journey.

God ever so gently applied the healing
oil of His knowledge and love by using those around me.
This, I learned, is why friends and supporters are so
important in my life, for it's through them, God I can see.

I can see now that as God so tenderly
cleansed and removed the infectious part of the wounds,
all the time He was doing this He was
creating a song in my heart which made my life more in tune.

He replaced and filled each wound
with new beautiful healthy parts of Himself like joy,
peace, long suffering, patience, and other
fruits of the Spirit of which I and those around me enjoy.

All that remains now are tiny pink
scars reminding me of the pain I had to face.
All that remains now are tiny pink
scars reminding me of God's matchless grace.

My Heavenly Father

October 8, 1994

To my loving Heavenly
Father, I will always be His little girl.
I can always come to Him
when I'm hurt by something in this world.

I can come to Him as the
needy helpless little child that I sometimes am.
He always greets me with
a sweet smile and never with a sour cold frown.

He will take me safely into
His strong powerful protecting arms,
as He assures me He is here
to comfort me through all life's harms.

He says He won't always prevent
the pain that will surely come my way,
But He will certainly be right
there in it with me anytime night or day.

I remember Him telling me that pain
was a teacher from which lessons I would learn.
I wondered if each different new pain
would bring a different lesson for me to discern.

Imagine my surprise when He, with patience
looked at me, this little child so trusting, so unknowing,
as He said, "it's the same lesson my child to
teach you to depend on me as your spiritual part is growing."

It seems awesome that He has been
here all the time to meet my dependency needs.
I need not depend on others in an
unhealthy way for He takes care of me as He hears my pleas.

My doting Heavenly Father treats
me like I'm His only special child when I pray,
and yet I know we all belong to
Him and He loves each of us in a unique way.

Because of my delight in Him,
my Heavenly Father is filled with joy and mirth.
He only wants good and happiness
for me as I journey through this life here on earth.

When I forget to listen to His voice, make
wrong choices and the mistakes follow soon after,
I fear no punishment as I accept the
responsibility, make amends, and learn from my teacher.

The only fear I have for my Heavenly Father
is awe, reverence, admiration, and worshipfulness.
This comes from the knowledge I've gained
from His undying love and unchanging graciousness.

With all my heart, soul and mind, I love
my compassionate adoring Heavenly Father so Divine.
I'm thankful that through the spirit of
adoption He chose me to be His and Himself to be mine.

Thank You Father

The Difference

October 9, 1994

The Difference A Word Makes

I was puzzled as I wrote the following:

In the sentences of life, God provides the subject and verb. He then allows me to choose the adjectives and adverbs. For more clarity He adds an occasional prepositional phrase and holds it all together with the conjunctions which connects me to Him.

In the sentence of life, I choose the subject and verb. God adds the adjectives and adverbs. For more clarity God adds an occasional prepositional phrase and holds it all together with the conjunctions which connects me to Him.

As I read this over and over again, I ask God, "which way is it?"
So patiently, He said, "it is both ways."
Still confused, I asked Him, " but how can that be, Father?"
He said, "my child, you have left off the most important word of all. Look at the difference the sentences read when you add as the first word of both: **SOMETIMES**"

The Difference A Letter Makes

Have you ever thought of the importance of the letters, U and I ?

If there were no I, there would be no ideas, no ideals, no identification, no illumination, no illustrator, no illustrations, no imagination, no importance, no improvements, no

Incarnation, no independence, no individuality, no information, no inspiration, no instinct, no insight, no intellect, no intimacy, no intuition, no I, and etc.

If there were no U there would be no ultimacy, no unabashed, no unashamed, no unbeaten, no unbelievable, no unblamableness, no unbreakable, no unchangeable, no unconditional, no uncriticalness, no unction, no undeniableness, no understanding, no undertakings, no undiscovered, no undreamed, no unfailing, no unforgettable, no fun, no sun, and no YOU.

If there were no U and I there would be no UNION or no UNITY.

The Observer

October 15, 1994

I look in the mirror and observe that some things are familiar, yet different.

The hair is about the same color, maybe cut just a little shorter in a more attractive style.

The skin, with the wrinkles, is the same except maybe a little lighter thanks to the new color of make up.

The eyes are different, but I can't catch what it is.

The mouth, too is not quite the same. It's more curved. It smiles more.

I observe my body unclothed. I'm not repulsed or think it unattractive. My waist is smaller, my hips have more curve, my stomach smaller, my legs are firmer. Though far from perfect, whatever that is, I'm happy with it.

I observe my body clothed. The older clothes that I like, hang loose. The new clothes that I've recently bought are a different style, brighter colors, and two sizes smaller. I feel pretty which I have not been able to do since I was thirteen.

I no longer need the layers of protection that I've needed before. I can now safely let them go.

I keep looking at the eyes. What is it that's so different?

I turn from the mirror and start straightening my room. As I pick up a book I notice my nails. Until about four months ago, they had been bitten to a nub. I remember one day at work I was looking at them and I mentioned to God how nice it would be to have long nails this fall. I knew working, my hands were very visible. I observed a few weeks later that I wasn't biting my nails any longer. It's been over four months now and I've treated myself to real manicures.

As I keep straightening up, I hear humming. I only recognize it is coming from me as it turns into singing. I listened to it. I realize I feel happy. I feel joy. I feel peace.

The phone rings and I hear myself answer with a chipper, "Good Morning." As I listen to the one sided conversation, I hear something new in this voice. It's not the compassion, for it's always been there. I don't think it's the love, though it sounds more free and more real. I hear laughter. I hear words like: Miracles, God Deals, Hope, Encouragement, Strength, Power, Healing, and Thankfulness. As I hang up the phone, I hear me say, "Father, thank you for friends. Remind all of us to listen to your voice."

My husband tells me that it occurs to him that we are communicating better. He says he feels that I really listen to him. He says he feels that when I talk I'm really expressing my opinions and not just saying what I think he wants to hear.

I had noticed, too that I don't fear his disapproval. I don't fear losing him or his love. I don't feel insecure. I'm not afraid to share my feelings, my opinions, or my beliefs with him. I can now ask questions. I can ask for what I want and need. It's okay if we disagree. It's okay if we are angry.

I'm aware that I no longer need someone's approval to know I'm okay. I no longer need someone else to "make" me feel loved, happy, or special. I have found all that within myself.

I observe that my fears are minimal. Because of the power within, I need not fear other's power. They can only affect me as I allow. It's my choice how much of my power, I'm willing to give up. It's my choice how open my boundaries are.

I observe that when I drove downtown Dallas the other day, I was calm even though I had missed my street. Considering that in the twenty eight years, I've lived here, I have only driven downtown about five times and each time I left a basket case and in tears, this time was radically different. This time there was excitement as I was chanting, "I'm driving downtown and I'm not afraid and I feel good." (Maybe that's why I missed my turn.)

As I glance in the mirror while walking by, I catch the eyes again. What is it that's so different about the eyes?

As I linger at the mirror for another second observing the reflection, I hear myself say, "I really love you. You are so special. Though I don't know you very well yet, I'm getting use to the changes, and I know I love you and I'm glad you are finally here."

As the reflection smiled back at me, I knew what it was. I knew what was different about the eyes. I saw no pain from the past. I saw no tears of grief for that lost childhood. I saw no frighten lonely little girl. Instead I saw a glowing light that was kept lit by reverence. I saw self confidence. I saw a hunger for knowledge. I saw Peace and calmness. I saw such a depth of love for myself and others. And JOY, Lord was there ever joy. Oceans and oceans of joy. I saw a strong courageous knowledgeable adult. I saw purpose and a desire to fulfill that purpose. I desired more than anything to share my knowledge and experience of hope, encouragement, and healing with others.

The difference I observed was the knowledge of the miracle of the Grace of God working in my life.

Yes, I Believe In Miracles

It's Hard to Believe

October 28, 1994

It's hard to believe when
the sky comes crashing all around me.
It's hard to believe when the
presence of God I can not feel, hear, or see.

It's hard to believe when there's
no feelings of strength, hope, joy, or peace.
It's hard to believe when the
tormenting thoughts in my head won't cease.

It's hard to believe as I hold
these two bottles of pills in my hand.

It's hard to believe as I persistently
keep trying to remember and understand.

It's hard to believe as the
tug of war goes on in my mind.
It's hard to believe when
the reason for living I can not find.

It's hard to believe as the cold
lonely damp blackness around me I feel.
It's hard to believe when this inside
torment reminds me there is more to heal.

It's hard to believe as I reach
out to others and they're not there.
It's hard to believe as I feel
so alone, unloved, and no one cares.

It's hard to believe as I
continue to clutch these bottles so tight.
It's hard to believe that
some how I could make it through the night.

It's hard to believe as my Father
reminds me of His strength like a tower.
It's hard to believe that dwelling
within me is the One who has such power.

It's hard to believe my Heavenly
Father really is here to watch and protect.
It's hard to believe there are those
that still don't know and this gift they reject.

It's hard to believe that I can
sit here and rejoice in the pain I was in.
It's hard to believe it's the same
lesson I'm learning as He teaches again.

Where There's No Love

November 7, 1994

Where there's no love,
there is a bottomless empty pit.
Where there's no love,
there are no pieces that seem to fit.

Where there's no love,
there is no warmth, just a chill.
Where there's no love,
there is an empty void not filled.

Where there's no love,
there are no feelings of joy or peace.
Where there is no love,
there is a pain that will never cease.

Where there's no love,
there are no sounds of care free laughter.
Where there's no love,
there is no hope for today or the day after.

Where there's no love,
there is a never ending strife.
Where there's no love,
there is no purpose in this life.

Where there's no love,
there is no God.
Where there's no God,
there is no love.

My Passion

November 12, 1994

My heart beats within my breast with
an invigorating passion I've never known.
With every heart beat it swells with love
for my God and for the Grace He has shown.

With every beat this passion for
life overwhelms me to the point of tears.
I feel something Holy is growing
within me, something that casts out all fears.

With every beat this new passion
brings with it more strength and more power.
It removes doubt, fear, and disbelief
that shows its face sometimes in a lonely hour.

I feel like little Mary excited with the
Holy secret she kept as the Holy Birth drew near.
People didn't know the miracle taking place,
this Holy Baby growing inside whom she loved so dear.

She knew her son would not belong to her.
Her purpose was to share Him with all mankind.
I wonder if she thought of this often or did
she choose to push those thoughts from her mind.

I wonder if she felt the passion from the honor
of being chosen to be used by God in this unique way.
I wonder if she really understood the gift of love
she was giving and receiving for the price she would pay.

As this passion continues to beat steadfast
within me, with each miraculous pounding heart beat,
I know though this life is difficult and painful
sometimes, I no longer will have to cry out in defeat.

As this passion takes over, love abounds for
everyone and everything that my life touches each day.
It's as if I've been set free to love and receive
love as I compassionately see God's creations in a new way.

Keep the Channels Open

November 13, 1994

God's love has no earthly boundaries or time tables. He gives
it freely and allows it to flow at will.
As it flows through us to others, we have no control whether
it's accepted or not, though it won't lie still.

We are only to be concerned with being that willing
channel to others as His love smoothly, gently, and
harmoniously flows.
Our responsibility is to keep the channel clean and free
of things that would clog it, keeping His love from where it
chooses to go.

As He allows us to share the knowledge of our experiences,
He loves, comforts, and encourages others through us.

He's revealing to them they are not alone, there is a way to get
through the pain as a Higher Power they learn to trust.

In order to keep our channel open to others, it is most
important that we keep our own channel to and from God
clear.
It's when we choose to listen to His voice and receive His
wisdom that we will keep the channels open as His Miracles
of Grace we declare.

Lines and Wrinkles

November 13, 1994

This poem was inspired by the beautiful photograph of Barbara Bush on the cover of her book, *Barabra Bush, A Memoir*. Though I've never met her, I feel she exhibits the kind of love I'm learning about so I choose to dedicate this poem to her.

Beautiful faces carved with
lines and wrinkles have a special story to tell.
Each one different and
represents a stage of life clearly defined as well.

They tell stories of tragedies
heartaches, losses, disappointments and pain.
Stories of fears, doubts, making
mistakes, and those goals of ours not attained.

Some are cut deep within our
skin like ruts that have dried in a road.
Some are thinner measuring
the heaviness or lightness of our load.

The laugh lines around the eyes
seem to tell completely different contrasting stories.
Life wasn't all bad, all sorrow and
pain. These lines show other noticeable categories.

There were laughter, joy, and
grace mixed in to balance life's scales.
There were gifts of miracles
sprinkled in to calm the stormy gales.

I think wrinkles and lines are full
of individuality and special kind of beauty.
They are a testimonial we've weathered
growing up and have now reached maturity.

Every Labor of Love Gives Birth to a Miracle

November 14, 1994

I thank God for your beauty from within
which radiates through your caring eyes;
reminding me of the eyes of an angel, showing
forth compassion and love again and again.

I thank God for your beauty from within
which soothes through your soft voice so
strong with words of hope, encouragement,
and wisdom that seem to never end.

I thank God for your beauty from within
which comes with your gentle smile that

says," I see another miracle. I see healing
taking place where it's never been."

I ask God daily to continue filling you with
His beauty as His love flows through those
who touch your life as well as those whose
lives you touch.

I ask God to give you more of His
knowledge as you so artfully and lovingly
share with others in their pain who
need it so much.

I ask God to fill you to overflowing
with more miracles of joy, peace, and strength
as you are blest to be someone's
temporary crutch.

I ask God to love you for me.

My Christmas Prayer

November 27, 1994

Thank you, Father, for your grace that
allowed the way to You, through your Son.
Into the world He willingly came as an
expression of Your love to each and everyone.

I pray that our lives may be the same
expression, as we journey along the way,
of Your unconditional love which You
are sending through us into the world today.

As we learn to accept, forgive
and lovingly touch the lives of others,
may this be our expression of
our love to You, our Heavenly Father.

My Dress

February 8, 1995

Everyone may not can see the beauty
that is in this tiny yellowed dress all tattered and torn.
I see the beauty of love and faith from my Sis
who loved and gave me my name, even before I was born.

For over forty eight painful years we had to
be apart, and it was safely kept in my Sis' loving care.
It reminded her of me and kept me close
to her heart as the grief for our loss she had to bear.

She had kept it knowing one day she would
give it back to me for she believed it was in God's plans.
The day had come and we experienced a miracle
when with tears of joy she gently placed it in my hands.

She was returning the dress to me for God had so
graciously returned us to each other and our lives He blest.
Everyone around us believed in miracles that day
as we embraced again and I clutched my beautiful baby dress.

What's the Next Step, Father?

March 7, 1995

What's the next step, Father on
this exciting marvelous journey of mine?
What are you going to teach me
today as the yesterdays I leave behind?

Where will the next step take
me, Father and with whom will I share?
Who will I meet taking this journey
with me that needs reminding that you care?

I look back at where you've
brought me, with thanksgiving in my heart.
I can remember the pain and fear
within me and the courage it took to start.

What's the next step, Father?
I feel that I am some place I've never been.
I like it here and wonder how long
I'll get to stay before my steps start again.

It seems funny as I think about, in
the middle of pain, I pray for joy and peace,
and then when I'm receiving them,
I'm asking how much longer before they cease?

For Lisa, with Love

March 7, 1995

I ask God sometime back why
He didn't bless us with a special poem for you.
He told me I hadn't ask for one.
I wish I had known sooner this was all I had to do.

Well Lisa, I guess the time has
come to leave the safety and warmth of this nest.
I know the time is right and
because of my healing and growth it's for my best.

I appreciate the fact that you,
with respect, allowed me to choose the day and time.
I appreciate that you allowed
me in the driver's seat for this spiritual journey of mine.

You have been an insightful
patient navigator and guide on this journey we've shared.
I am taking so much of you
with me, but of all the gifts, thanks for showing you cared.

I still have a difficult time putting
my potpourri of feelings into the spoken word.
How do I say thanks for helping
me get well so I can fly off like a scared little bird?

How do I explain the feelings of
empowerment, strength, courage, and confidence
while at the same time I am shaking
like a leaf on the inside yet outwardly there's no evidence?

I'm wondering, dear Lisa, if this is
maybe just another one of those confusing paradox things.
You know, the more you give away,
the more that comes back or if you're unhappy, just sing.

I think what's really glorious is that
I'm sitting here braced for the worst kind of pain
and what I'm feeling is so much joy,
Peace, and love because of knowledge I've gained.

When our Heavenly Father blesses me with pleasant thoughts
and memories of what we shared,
I'll know it's a reminder of His Grace in our lives and for you,
I will thank Him with a simple prayer.

We have learned that for healing to take place in someone's
confused mind, it must come from within.
You are blest to have the awesome responsibility for caring for
someone's soul as their journey they begin.

I ask Him to remind you, when you are caring for wounded
souls, to pray, asking for His wisdom and Grace.
I ask Him to gently remind you of Himself when you think of
me and the miracles we've seen take place.

Dearest Lisa, I ask God that with each
new challenge to please give you peace with His wisdom.
I ask Him to give you courage as you listen and follow your
intuitiveness which is a gift from Him.

I ask Him to somehow let you
receive the hugs that I want to send your way.
And if you feel a touch on your
cheek, it's just an angel reassuring you, I'm okay.

I have no doubt that in our Spirit
we'll never be more than an angel's wing apart.
God provides a beautiful gift called
memories allowing us to visit within our hearts.

Thanks for the, "I'm wondering...,"
and the, "What would Lisa say or suggest I do?"
It's with mixed emotions that I can
boldly say, "Lisa, thanks for my no longer needing you."

Happy Birthday, Lisa

March 14, 1995

Lisa, I celebrate the wondrous
day, the miraculous gift of your birth.
The day God lovingly let you go,
and sent you to live here on this Earth.

I can only imagine the joy of
those who prepared to welcome you.
I wonder if they were blest to
recognize the other miracles that came, too.

I want to celebrate the awesome
gift of your blessed spiritual birth as well.
For what ever the reason, with
child like faith you chose heaven over hell.

With the same faith, I feel you
have accepted your unique purpose for being.
I celebrate the miracles you've
experienced and in others you are now seeing.

I celebrate because you were
chosen to help guide me to find the bridge.
I celebrate that in faith I was able
to cross over instead of jumping over the edge.

I celebrate, with you, each day
He gives you His Wisdom to peacefully live.
I celebrate that through you, to
others, His love and guidance He is able to give.

I celebrate the wondrous
day, the miraculous gift of your birth.
The day God, with love, knowing
you would return, sent you to live on earth.
Happy Birthday and Everyday

A Celebration of Life is.....

March 26, 1995

A celebration of ignorance and knowledge.
A celebration of confusion and insight.
A celebration of pain and growth.
A celebration of fear and courage.
A celebration of doubt and belief.
A celebration of miracles and gifts.

A celebration of choices and responsibilities.
A celebration of mistakes and forgiveness.
A celebration of hopelessness and purpose.
A celebration of losses and recreating.
A celebration of excessiveness and balance.
A celebration of emptying and refilling.

*A celebration of the right to march to our own drummer.
A celebration of the right to extend ourselves to others.
A celebration of the right to accept or refuse this gift.
A celebration of the right to search and reclaim.
A celebration of the right to choose to not live with only
second hand, hand me down, and borrowed knowledge.*

*A celebration of learning something isn't real.
A celebration of asking what is real.
A celebration of searching for what is real.
A celebration of finding and knowing what is real.
A celebration of acknowledging what is real.
A celebration of sharing what is real.*

*A celebration of God's love, which just like the sun that
keeps shinning behind a cloud, knows no boundaries.
It's there whether we can, with our eyes, see it or not.
It's there whether we choose to accept it or not.
It's there whether we believe it or not.
It's there because it is real.*

The Fragrance of Love

April 13, 1995

*Crush a clove of garlic
or the petals of a dew kissed rose.
The powerful fragrance
intoxicates us as it drifts to our nose.*

*Crush the selfishness of
God's pure love and watch it grow.*

Its fragrance comes not from
feelings, but from what we know.

The fragrance, as it fills our
senses, brings miracles to our soul.
It brings healing, peace, and
joy as we trust God with this control.

The fragrance of this awesome
love is to be shared for God's delight.
This is possible when our heart
He gently crushes as we walk in His light.

The fragrance that emerges is
richer and fuller than all others known.
This is permitted to take place as
we learn and our spiritual part has grown.

My Morning Awareness

April 22, 1995

Father, I know I'll have
choices throughout the day to make.
I ask your wisdom with
each one as to which direction to take.

I know the choices are mine
and I will accept the responsibilities.
My own knowledge is limited
because I don't see all the possibilities.

I can only see today, this hour,
this circumstance, this storm with the rain.
In confusion I ask, "how could you
let this happen, why all this terrible pain?"

You are the one able to see and
know the whole plan for our lives here.
You see the whole picture, not
just the bits and pieces here and there.

It's through the pain and confusion
I'm able to learn as my spiritual part grows.
Instead of asking, "why," remind me
to ask, "what are you wanting me to know?"

Because of who you are and who
I am in You, I trust you with my life and soul.
After all, You gave me both for your
pleasure so I know you will help keep me whole.

I have no anxiety for the yesterdays,
the today or even the future and what it holds.
I trust your Fatherly love for me, which is
boundless, free, everlasting and never grows old.

It's because of this knowledge
I can face, with joy and anticipation, each day.
It's because of this knowledge
that I can walk in your light which lights my way.

Humanity, Humanity

April 28, 1995

Humanity, Humanity,
why do you continue
to try to destroy the Spirit
of God that dwells within you?

Unfold your arms of
ignorance and apathy
and open them to knowledge
of your own spiritual reality.

One by one remove
the learned boundaries,
the cold, high, stone walls
that keep you from being free.

Experience the feelings
of despair and helplessness
and then accept the serenity
of God's grace and goodness.

Examine your feelings
of fear, hate, and unbelief.
With new knowledge you'll
begin to enjoy peace and relief.

With knowledge you
will learn to replace them
with security, Love, and
trust that comes only from Him.

With knowledge you
will learn to look within
and listen to your inner
voice as your new growth begins.

You'll find no need to
follow others and their views,
as you follow the directions
that come from within you.

You'll find it takes a lot
of courage to make this choice.
It's easier to follow someone
else instead of your own inner voice.

Before, if things didn't
work out well, you felt no shame
for you trusted and followed
someone else, so they were to blame.

I have found so much
more freedom when I choose.
With God's help it's my choice
so it doesn't matter if I win or lose.

This freedom allows me
to learn from all circumstances.
This knowledge comes from
looking within, not just little glances.

If we lack love, courage,
knowledge or it's hard to believe,
God is ready to teach all the
above when we are ready to receive.

So looking deep within,
what choice will you make?
Will you follow others or your
own responsibility will you take?

In all things give thanks
and you'll find joy each day.
In all thy ways acknowledge
God and He will direct your way.

You and Yours

May 4, 1995

With all the smiles I receive
each day, there's still one missing.
It's yours.

With all the hugs I receive every
now and then, there's still one missing.
It's yours.

With all the voices I hear around
me, still there's one I yearn to hear.
It's yours.

With all the people that are gifts
in my life, still someone is missing.
It's you.

With all the miracles happening
around me, there's one I want to embrace.
It's you.

I lost to soon what I didn't get
to have long enough to really know.
It's you.

My heart aches, I'm sick with
love and there's only one sure cure.
It's you.

There's one that I thank God for
every time I'm blest when you visit my mind.
It's you.

Songs of the Bird

July 2, 1995

God speaks through the
winsome songs of the bird.
Everywhere, no matter
where we are, He can be heard.

Their melodious songs
are there to continually remind
that He is forever with
us our tangled lives to help unwind.

Through their songs He
speaks of love, joy, peace, and hope.
The songs they sing are
like none that mortal man ever wrote.

On this journey of life if
we forget the promises of His word,

He's there to sweetly remind
us through the songs of the bird.

Pain is My Friend

August 2, 1995

We've become good
buddies. Pain is my friend.
I see him often because
he comes again and again.

We're very familiar now.
We're even on first name basis.
I leave the door unlock, but if
I'm not home, after me he chases.

My friend, pain, is very
dependable. I don't even have to call.
He seems to always know when
to come as my feelings begin to thaw.

Pain is my friend. He's forever
bringing new knowledge through lessons I learn.
He's always making me grow
stronger as new courage and confidence I earn.

I feel bad for the times wasted
before I accepted him as my friend.
All I wanted was for him to
go away so the challenges would end.

It took a long time to learn
that he wasn't there to make me die.
It took a long time to accept
him as a friend and stop asking why.

Now, because he's my friend, I'm aware
he'll forever be a part of this life of mine.
When he appears I look, with courage,
to see what he's brought to teach me this time.

As the new knowledge is internalized
and becomes wisdom, my friend disappears.
However, he always leaves me with special
gifts of joy and peace in place of my tears.

Soul Mates

September 2 - October 29, 1995

A soul yearns for a soul mate to
learn and grow with and to share a life unending.
A soul longs for a soul mate
whose spiritual values and beliefs are unbending.

A soul, housed in a body made from
the dust of the earth, remembers what it already knows.
A soul, within a frail human form, sure
of its power and strength as through knowledge it shows.

A soul mysteriously searches for
attachment yet at the same time needs to be free.
Beautifully clothed with its fantasies
and dreams, perfection it does not have to see.

Like the warmth of the sunshine,
one's smile can brighten the grayest of days.
In times of confusion, one can give a
hug that says, "everything's gonna be okay."

In times of discouragement, sadness,
losses, and other pain causing unbearable grief,
someone can be there with comforting
words or maybe just their presence brings relief.

Maybe it's the joy and pleasure one
receives just quietly sitting alone with another.
No words need be spoken or actions
taken, as intimacy passes from one to the other.

Maybe it's the laughter from deep
within that can be seen in the twinkle of one's eyes
that stirs thanksgiving and awe in the
heart of another, like seeing the rainbow in the skies.

Maybe it's the mysterious strong
bond between two souls that can't be explained
that comes from the creator Himself
that enables each in their heart this love to claim.

Whose soul is searching for this
miracle. Who has this void needing to be filled?
Who has the courage to take
the risk so the winds of the soul at last are stilled?

Who will risk the awkwardness of
their imperfections to be seen and known
just so the miracle of love and the
humbling lessons of forgiveness can be shown?

Who will choose to break loose from
the ropes of the shoulds and should nots?
Who chooses to be free as the winds of
two souls softly blow together, never to stop?

Who, with fear, will find the courage
to remove the boundaries that keep another away.
Who will choose to enjoy the warmth
of another, by listening to what their soul has to say?

Who will know the gift of embracing
while being embraced and of giving while receiving?
Who will experience the gift of inviting
while being invited, and of being loved while loving?

In creating our own happiness,
in taking responsibility for our own lives,
is this a miracle we've always been
blest with only it has been lying in disguise?

They say that the losses we experience
are the price that we pay for the privilege to live.
They say that feeling whole and complete can
only come as to others a part of ourselves we give.

They say that every day as we are learning
how to live, at the same time we are already dying.
It's when we think maybe we have a grip on
this thing called life that too fast we find time is flying.

I wonder how many soul mates have been
needlessly cast aside out or ignorance or fear?
I wonder if it is because of denial of our
own soul's yearning that we won't let them near?

Our time here is to short to not heed
the passion of our soul as we continue to grow.
Time is to short to deny the gift of love
through that special soul mate God wants to bestow.

My Prayer for Peace in Life

December 11, 1995

Father, how can we expect peace in the
world if we lack peace in our heart, soul or mind?
How can there be peace in our homes or
schools if within our own selves we remain so blind?

Father, in this game of life, please remind
us there is no longer need for competition or war.
It's only with knowledge and wise choice
making that makes the need for conflict no more.

In leaving behind an exquisite portrait
of our perception of You when we vacate this earth,
let us have so deliberately painted in your
captivating eyes the look of peace, love, and mirth.

Father, please remind us of your law of cause
and effect every time we hear the winds start to blow.
Please remind us as the storms of life start to
come, that our "peace be still" lies in what we know.

Thank you for the highest honor to be an
instrument of your Peace in the orchestra of life.
We no longer wish to choose to be an out
of tune instrument of discord and sounding of strife.

Father, as we sing, "Let there be Peace on
earth and let it begin in me," may it ring loud and clear.
After all, isn't this the same lesson of love and
forgiveness that Jesus taught and lived while He was here?

Give us the wisdom to show forth this
Christ of love and peace in our own lives this season.
For this life long task, to share this hope,
for being on this earth, this is the ultimate reason.

My Eulogy to Ervin Middlebrooks

December 18, 1995

In celebration of the
wondrously changed life of a man
on whose own two feet,
for the longest, he could not stand.

His shoes would be hard
to fill, if we thought we could.
For years now, they were
filled with feet made of wood.

This life, tho tainted in the
past with pain and imperfections,
became new, and graced with
change, courage, and inspiration.

A noteworthy lesson can
be learned by all that knew him.
Some changes just happen,
while others, we can choose them.

We each learn to face the
circumstances of life that appear.
We can choose to do it
with love and courage, or choose fear.

So in the times when the
shoes are hard to fill or we sense defeat,
if we don't feel strong, just
ask, and God will give us two new feet.

Peg Leg's voice will be missed
by many down here over the CB waves,
but at the same time, his life will be
remembered as in our hearts he forever stays.

I'm reminded that tho the
heavenly air waves are not the same,
God's CB is lots stronger
and all we have to do is call His name.

With joy, I'm gonna sign off
now with a big ten four, I suppose,
In celebration, of knowing
the man who called me Dusty Rose.

Good-bye Ninety Five

December 31, 1995

Another year has swiftly and quietly past
while knowledge was confidently being gained.
Again so much has happened, making my
life a miracle and to never again be the same.

So many needed healthy changes were
made as the fears were courageously faced.
A lot of growing, and learning had to
be done so continual healing could take place.

As usual the changes did not come
easily and there was pain that I befriended.
There were moments, before making my
choice to grow up, that my life nearly ended.

I had to choose to want to leave the
familiar role of the helpless dependent child victim.
God showed me that part of my self,
mirrored in others and then I just wanted to run.

God, using a wise feisty red headed
stick of dynamite whose name is DiannaLynn,
blasted me once and for all over the
hump in the road where I had so long been.

The blast did more than either one of
us had thought or dreamed could have been done.
It made such a deep gorge in the road
behind me that there was no where back there to run.

It was through this, another miracle,
that I was taught I could leave that role behind.
It had served its purpose in my life,
my eyes were opened and I was no longer blind.

I remember writing last New Year's Day
that I was going to strive to be alive in ninety five.
I look back today and have to weep with
joy because I know what it feels like to be alive.

Presently it seems that I fall in love
with something new each and every day.
Sometimes it's the author of the book
I'm currently reading or a picture by Monet.

I've fallen in love with wisdom and
my life daily, since I met Mr. Emerson.
I've fallen in love with my joyful self,
while getting to know Emily Dickenson.

I've had to learn first hand about
the kind of love that lets some things go.
I don't have to explain or justify
my life to anyone, for God and I know.

God loves mysteries and so do I.
He's a humorist, just look at His paradox.
He gives us this precious gift of
life but not in a neatly wrapped little box.

We can have all the love we want,
but to get it, we have to keep giving it away.
To love someone we may have to let
them go for their good and not make them stay.

Yes, a lot of beautiful lessons were
learned in this year that so quickly has passed.
Next year these challenges will all
be memories, but the wisdom in my soul will last.

My Joy

January 5, 1996

Sometimes it seems that
my joy is clouded by the dark pain.
I know it will pass and
soon the joy is all that will remain.

I know, in my soul, that
the joy never really leaves me.
It's just with the cloud of
pain it becomes harder to see.

I'm reminded once more
that the sun does always shine.
It's just that behind the
clouds, we can't see it all the time.

Again, I'm learning I can't
go by my human feelings alone.
I'm thankful for the
knowledge of the "faith seeds" sown.

I'm thankful for these little
exercises that help my faith grow.
I'm thankful for the experiences,
reminding me of what I do know.

It's times like this that my
soul muscles grow, becoming stronger.
That's the pain I feel; the
tightening, making them weak no longer.

As I conscientiously search
daily for God's knowledge and wisdom,
I am exercising my faith by
nurturing my soul and more joy will come.

I'm aware that my joy doesn't
come and go like the seasons of the year.
It's steadfast and sure just like
the knowledge that the joy giver is near.

My Angels

January 16, 1996

My loneliness swiftly disappears
as before me ministering angels appear.

"With joy I welcome you all here
as the peace song you sing loud and clear.

Some people might think it queer
as from the norm I courageously veer.

While some might laugh and jeer
I'm the one who's experiencing you here.

I feel your divine presence so near
as your soft wings brush away my tears.

With understanding let me hear
as your words of wisdom fall on my ears.

The words you speak are so dear
as they consistently calm my human fears."

My loneliness swiftly disappears
as before me ministering angels appear.

For DiannaLynn, with Love

January 16, 1996

It's really my therapist's fault,
you know. She's at least partly to blame.
Because of her pushing and her
challenging, my life won't ever be the same.

She refused to allow me to continue
in the frightened helpless child victim role.
Instead, she blasted me over that blasted
hump, so my life I could learn to take control.

It was so scary. I knew she just
didn't understand the hell I found myself in.
But, I guess she really did know and
that's why a new life she wanted me to begin.

It's really my therapist's fault,
you know. She's at least partly to blame.
Thanks to her pushing and her
challenging, my life won't ever be the same.

This World Is Not My Home

January 25-30, 1996

I'm not from around here.
I'm from a different far away place.
I'm only here for a short time.
I came to learn as I run in life's race.

One day, many light years ago
from many many light years away,
God ask for volunteers to come
to earth and sow seeds along the way.

The plan sounded pretty simple.
I would come to earth as a little baby girl.
I would grow up as a human, but
remembering I was not really of this world.

I would have painful human
experiences from which I would learn
who I was, where I came from
and what I needed to know to return.

I've learned that everyone here
has the same purpose, the same quest.
I've learned that we aren't alone
as we are striving to do our very best.

We are all spiritual volunteers
representing God on this planet earth.
We all have our lessons to learn
as we grow into our perfect spiritual worth.

God sent an example before us
Who was known as the "Way Show-er."
He, too, lived as a human with
the task to not only teach, but much more.

He gave His life for what He
believed and thus returned to His home.
Remembering that He was our
example, are we to do less with our own?

Could the mystery, the big
secret be so simple that we just can't see?
Could this be one of the times
we are unable to see the forest for the trees?

God gives us a "free will" to
choose which way we want to live.
He gives us lots of options as
we learn what we want to keep or give.

As humans we only see in bits
and pieces of the challenges around us.
We experience the pain and
suffering as punishment for our wickedness.

As we learn and grow, we will
see things differently, through God's eyes.
He looks at us as only part of the
big picture of life which He alone designs.

We can go about life in our
human ways trying to make it on our own.
Listening to our ego and making
choices that bring suffering from seeds sown,

Or we can choose to exchange
our will for His and ask for His wisdom, too.
It's with this knowledge we learn to
receive more peace and joy than we ever knew.

It's through the renewal of our
minds that this transformation can begin.
We learn that God is the only
power in this universe and He lives within.

Belief and faith are all that we
will ever need while we are journeying here.
When we believe and live as if
God is in control, there is no other to fear.

The experiences we have are
created by our own minds as we perceive.
Depending on what we need to
learn on this journey is what we will receive.

We are lovingly welcomed here as
students who are anxious to grow and learn.
It isn't too long before we find that
we, too, have become teachers and it's our turn.

My Old Acquaintances

February 3, 1996

Three familiar acquaintances, Anger,
Rejection, and Abandonment, came to call.
Unlike before, I didn't slam the door
in their faces, instead I welcomed them all.

The visit was much different this
time as we all sat down and shared tea.
I sat with open heart and mind to
see what wisdom they had brought to me.

Our visit was soon cut short
because there was another knock at my door.
I threw it open wide to find Love,
Joy, and Peace waiting to come visit once more.

Anger, Rejection, and Abandonment
quietly and politely excused themselves and left.
They muttered something about not
being needed anymore since I'd found my True Self.

I ask if they would be coming
back from time to time to visit or just say hello.
They said they would try, but
they had so many others to see, they didn't know.

Love, Joy, and Peace said they
could stay for as long as I wanted them here.
As we laughed and visited, time
was passing, and they asked when I last saw Fear.

I had to stop and think but couldn't
remember, I knew it had been quite a while.
I told them it had been a long time
since I had seen Pain, too, and we all smiled.

I told these friends that I thanked
God for their visits and wished to share them.
They said that would be great for
that was their purpose since they came from Him.

I want to encourage and inspire
everyone to open their door to Love, Joy, and Peace.
They are wonderful companions
sent to us from our Father so from worry we can cease.

Walking Miracles

February 27, 1996

I'm a walking miracle,
but are you any different than I?
Do we not both experience
merriment and do we both not cry?

You say life's a bitch and
you just have plain rotten bad luck.
You've been dealt a bad hand,
and thanks to your past, your life is stuck.

Do we both not awaken
to challenges and experiences each day?
Do we both not have choices
in our reactions of what to do or what to say?

When do we accept responsibility
for our life in this moment in the here and now?
When do we learn to take control
and call upon our power within to show us how?

For what purpose for what good
is served by remaining a helpless victim.
For what purpose for what good
is served by claiming a new life and freedom?

I'm a walking miracle,
but are you any different than I?
I have found my freedom,
by staring fear and ignorance in the eye.

Please come join with me
and let's walk as miracles side by side.
Together, we can be Way
Show-ers to others who in pain still hide.

We are walking miracles,
but are they any different from you and me?
They just haven't learned
the secret. The whole picture they can't see.

Now we know our purpose.
Now we see the good of our new life.
We are walking miracles
sharing our story to those still in strife.

When?

February 28, 1996

When does the student become the teacher?
When does the teacher become the student?
When does the child become the parent?
When does the parent become the child?
When does the weak become the stronger?
When does the stronger become the weak?
When does the victim become the survivor?
When does the survivor become the victim?
When does the one loving become loved?

When does the one loved become loving?
When does the stranger become a friend?
When does the friend become a stranger?
When does the poor become richer?
When does the richer become poor?

When does love give way to fear?
When does fear give way to love?
When does heaven become hell?
When does hell become heaven?
When does the water become ice?
When does the ice become water?
When does a miracle become a life?
When does a life become a miracle?
When does light turn into darkness?
When does darkness turn into light?

When do we see the glass half empty?
When do we see the glass half full?
When does knowledge grow from ignorance?
When does ignorance disappear for knowledge?
When do challenges become learning experiences?
When do learning experiences become challenges?

When will we remember?
When will we forget?

When will we know when?
When?

Most of All

(My Love Song to God)

March 4, 1996

Thank you, God, for eyes to see.
And thank you, God, for ears to hear.
But most of all, I thank thee,
most of all for you and me.

Thank you, God for hands to hold.
And thank you, God, for feet to go.
But most of all, I thank thee,
most of all, for you and me.

Thank you, God, for a heart of love.
And thank you, God, for your grace.
But most of all, I thank thee,
most of all, for you and me.

Thank you, God, for your peace.
And thank you, God, for your joy.
But most of all, I thank thee,
most of all, for you and me.

Thank you God!!!

The Dying Seed

March 14, 1996

I desire not to posses
only to bless as I am blest,
Nothing more, nothing less.

For seeds so lovingly sown,
I wish for others and not you alone,
to see and know how they've grown.

In my heart planted so deep,
they are nurtured as the vigil I keep,
until the appointed time comes to reap.

With the sun as well as the rain,
they germinate through joy and pain,
until spiritual maturity they attain.

I'm amazed how under layers of manure
the fruit can slowly grow and mature
and still somehow be fragrant and pure.

It's important that the area is weeded
and attention is given as needed
so that the growth isn't impeded.

The time of reaping is at last near,
but the one who sowed is not here,
to gather the fruits as they appear.

Maybe this is the way it should be,
tho it doesn't seem real fair to me,
to plant seeds and the fruit not see.

However, the loving owner of the field
still knows best no matter how I feel.
My desire, like the sower is to do His will.

My purpose, like the seed's, is to die
while on my Heavenly Father I learn to rely
as through me the fruits of His love multiply.

Spiritual Experiences

March 23, 1996

If you've ever smelled a perfect rose,
or heard the perfect song from a songbird,
If you've ever seen the perfect sunset,
or in the gentle wind, a voice faintly heard,

If you've tasted a juicy ripe strawberry,
or you've touched a baby's soft fragile skin,
if you've ever baked that perfect cake,
or if you've laughed and cried with a friend,

If you've ever tripped and fallen down
and somehow you found courage to get up,
If you've ever felt so much joy love and
peace that couldn't be contained in your cup,

If you've felt love or pain for people you don't know,
or if you've done "the right thing" and felt pride,
If you get a lump in your throat at the sight of the flag,
or while singing " God Bless America," you've cried,

Then you, my friend, have experienced
a Power that's higher than any other.
You have had a spiritual experience
with God, your spiritual Father/Mother.

Before

February 5 - June 10, 1996

Before a mountain top experience, I had to experience the wilderness.
Before the wilderness experience, I had to honor the desire to learn.

Before I knew the questions, God gave me the answers.
Before I knew what to ask for, I had the desire to know it.

Before I can teach, I must learn.
Before I can learn I have to be taught.

Before I could learn, I had to unlearn.
Before I could remember, I had to forget.

Before I can build the life I want, I must read the instructions.
Before I have an experience, I must not receive what I wanted.

Before knowledge, there was ignorance and fear.
Before ignorance and fear, there was abuse and neglect.

Before the knowledge of evil, there was innocence.
Before I could recover my innocence, I had to deny the power of evil.

Before I could gain access to the Kingdom of God, I had to become as a child.
Before I could become as a child, I had to deny knowledge of evil to experience innocence.

Before finding pearls of wisdom, I had to know where to look.
Before appreciating the beauty, I had to experience the ugly.

Before I could find Truth, I had to lose false beliefs.
Before I knew to lose false beliefs, I had to find Truth.

Before I can be set free, I must have Truth.
Before I receive Truth, I must be set free.

Before I could be free, I had to want to be free.
Before I could be healed, I had to want to be healed.

Before I could be free, I had to put aside or rid my Self of all the useless unnecessary baggage.
Before I could set aside the baggage, I had to look through it to separate what I wanted to keep.

Before I can believe, I must have faith.
Before I can have faith, I must believe.

Before I could believe, I had to see.
Before I could see, I had to believe.

Before there can be peace on this planet, there has to be peace within me.
Before there could truly be peace within me, I had to know the peace giver.

Before experiencing peace, I endured the storm.
Before enduring the storm, I had to have faith.

Before I could receive a new mind, I had to lose the old one.
Before I could be healed, I had to know I was in need of healing.

Before I could change my life, I had to change my mind.
Before I could change my mind, I had to change my life.

Before I can experience the positive, I must deny the negative.
Before I can deny the negative, I must experience the positive.

Before I could exhibit courage, I had to face fears.
Before I could face fears, I had to practice being courageous.

Before there is salvation, there had to be acceptance.
Before I could be clothed in righteousness, I had to become naked.

Before I could taste, I had to open my mouth.
Before I could open my mouth, I had to know it was good.

Before I could speak, I had to be silent.
Before I could be silent, I had to speak.

Before I could see, I had to become blinded.
Before I could become blinded, I had to see.

Before I could hear the quiet voice within, I had to be quiet and still.
Before hearing the small voice within, I had to cease from my own doings.

Before I could enjoy the sweet fragrance of the rose, it had to be crushed.
Before giving forth the sweet fragrance of God's love, I had to be willing.

Before touching that which is Holy, I had to become aware of the honor.

Before handling that which is Holy, I had to experience Love and worthiness.

Before I could love, I had to know Love.
Before I could know Love, I had to love.

Before I could be forgiven, I had to forgive.
Before I could forgive, I had to be forgiven.

Before I can receive, I must give.
Before I can give, I must receive.

Before I could celebrate a birthday, I had to be born.
Before I could be born, there was an expression of love.

Before I could celebrate life, I had to celebrate death.
Before I could celebrate death, I had to celebrate life.

Before I can sing, I must know the song.
Before I could know the song, I had to hear it.

Before I could appreciate joy, I had to entertain pain.
Before there can be an offering, there has to be a sacrifice.

Before I can lose something. I had to have had it.
Before I can let go of something, I had to have held it.

Before I can wake up, I must sleep.
Before there was light, there was darkness.

Before I could start, I had to stop.
Before I could live, I had to die.

Before the fruit of a harvest can be reaped, seeds must be sown.
Before the seeds could be planted the earth had to be made ready.

Before I can remember God, I must forget me.
Before I could experience miracles, I had to become one.

Before God can increase, I have to decrease.
Before being filled, I have to be emptied.

Before God can be the engine of my train, I must become the caboose.
Before I know where I'm going, I must know where I've been.

Before God can flow through me, the channels must be clear.
Before the channels can be clear, God must flow through me.

Before there is anything, there is an idea or thought.
Before I could receive a divine idea, I had to believe.

Before there was anything, God was.
Before there is anything, God is.

I Celebrate With You

May 15, 1996

In honor of the Fiftieth Wedding Anniversary Celebration of Mr. and Mrs. J. W. Russell, held Saturday, May 18, 1996.

On this your special golden
anniversary day, I honor and celebrate with you

the joy, as well as the tears, of
the memories of challenges you've come through.

I celebrate with you the knowledge
and strength that only those challenges could bring.
I celebrate with you the faith and
assurance in God and each other that continues to reign.

I celebrate with you the peace
and love you tirelessly seem to share
as daily you take the time to some
how show each other you really care.

I celebrate with you the awesome
wondrous gift of being devoted Soulmates.
The miracle of oneness with each other
and God is more than just learning to tolerate.

I celebrate with you in spirit as
friends and family lovingly gather around
to honor your fifty years together
and the joy, love, and peace you have found.

Grow Little Flowers, Grow

May 20, 1996

Grow little flowers, grow
as your beauty to the world you show.
Grow little flowers, grow
so that your Creator, others will know.

We are as the beautiful flowers
whether domesticated or growing wild and free.
We are sometimes the only beauty
of our loving Creator that others can see.

Thanks to those who were so
privileged to sow the seeds of love
that we might bloom here now
where we are, as through the soil we shoved.

Through necessary death and decay
of old thinking, beliefs and all the manure,
we, with courage and grit, pushed our
way up through it all as we learned to endure.

Now we can grow little flowers, grow
as our beauty to the world we joyfully show.
We can grow little flowers, grow
assured our Creator, others will see and know.

I'm Free, I'm Free

May 24, 1996

I saw a balloon that had
broken free from the bondage of its string.
As it floated so weightlessly
across the street I believe I heard it sing:

I'm free, I'm free, the string
can hold me back no more.
I'm free, I'm free, I'm no longer
in bondage so watch me soar.

As I watched the balloon aimlessly
floating and gently bumping into each car,
I thought how wonderful to be so free
and to be able to sing right where we are:

I'm free, I'm free, the string
can hold me back no more.
I'm free, I'm free, I'm no longer
in bondage so watch me soar.

Oh, to be able to take life's
little bumps with such carefree ease.
Just a soft touch and then sing
along as we float in the gentle breeze:

I'm free, I'm free, the string
can hold me back no more.
I'm free, I'm free, I'm no longer
in bondage so watch me soar.

In ignorance we have strings of
thoughts that keep us attached and bound.
Until a miracle happens and our spirit
breaks free and we sing of the joy we've found:

I'm free, I'm free, those old
strings can hold me back no more.
I'm free, I'm free, I'm no longer
in bondage so watch me bravely soar.

Waking Up

July 24, 1996

You say that your life is
difficult and it feels like a living hell.
You say nothing goes right and
you feel you're under someone else's spell.

You say it's one thing after
another that seems to bring you pain.
It's your bad health, accidents,
losses, or loved ones that drive you insane.

You say you can't find any
peace with so many decisions to make,
and your loved ones won't
listen as you point our their mistakes.

You say that you feel unloved and not
appreciated and you're not sure anyone cares.
You are always doing for others, but when it
comes to your needs for attention, it's never there.

You say you've spent your whole lifetime
being someone's child or someone's parent or spouse.
When is it your turn to be the artist, the
singer or the poet instead of feeling like a timid mouse.

You say your job is the pits
and you're stressed out at the end of the day.
But, you feel that you have to stay there
and endure because of the bills you have to pay.

You say you don't have many
friends that will sit and listen to you groan.
They seem so busy, guess they
might could have problems of their own.

You say you've learned to just
accept that life on earth is gonna stink.
But it's okay because you've got
some pills to help or you'll get another drink.

After all, this was the way
you learned from your loving family
to numb the pain and hide
the secrets so no one else could see.

You say you tried being religious
and going to church, but that didn't work very well.
All you heard was what a terrible
sinner you were and that you were heading straight for hell.

You say you've thought about
ending it all and taking your life.
Guess that would be one way
to get out from under all this strife.

You say you wonder why life has to
be this way or why you were dealt this hand.
You've noticed others who seem to have
it together and aren't standing on sinking sand.

You say it feels like something is
missing and there's a big empty space.
You wonder what was there
before and how and if it can be replaced.

You say you're feeling confused and
you don't understand what life is all about.
How does one take the step to learn
when within themselves they have so much doubt?

How does one learn the answer
when they don't know the questions to ask?
Where does one find the courage
to even attempt such an awesome task?

How does one start, all this
confusion from themselves to rid?
I think,
my dearest friend, you just did.

My Writings

July 30, 1996

I know not the difference
between prose, poems, or an essay.
I only write with passion
the words that my soul yearns to say.

Not allowing doubts and fear
of imperfection stand in my souls way,
I will deliver with an obsession
the rhythm as in my mind they play.

With abandonment of caring
whether this word goes or stays,
I let them flow wild and free
like the light seen in the sun's rays.

Where Are the Instructions?

August 26, 1996

With my birth certificate, there
was a mistake and no instructions came.
How will I ever learn to do life
right? Or does everyone do it the same?

With the disappearing of my
loving family and my joining a new one,
No instructions came on coping
with the feelings concerning what was done.

With the fear and excitement
of the first big day of going to school,
there were no instructions that
came to warn me of all the different rules.

With the consistent guilt and
shame from molestation and sexual abusing,
there were no instructions on
grieving my self worth, which I was losing.

With the first scary confused
day of my big signal of womanhood,
no instructions came as on
this exciting new threshold I stood.

With my marriage certificate,
again someone forgot the instruction book.
With no healthy role models, the
fantasy TV families became the places to look.

With the adventures of motherhood,
as I held that precious baby so tiny and new,
I looked everywhere and finally asked,
"didn't they send any instructions with you?"

With the gift of my precious
grandchildren, who brings me such joy,
I find, again, no instructions
included either with the girls or the boys.

With the start of the miraculous new
journey into my personal growth and recovery,
there were no instructions telling me
how to deal with the pain of each new discovery.

With almost a year passing since
the divorce, I'm just now starting to grieve.
Where's the instructions telling
me how to let go of the fantasies I believed?

With no instructions for life, I'm
constantly afraid I'll mess up and not do it right.
I ask my Self, "what's the worst
that could happen and my fears came to light?

What would happen with no
instructions to follow as I live each day?
Would I forget who I am,
why I'm here, and would I lose my way?"

As I was pondering on these
questions, I looked deep within for a clue.
Again, my Spirit was faithful as
He said, "the answers are found within you.

What if you were writing your own
instructions as you faced your unique experiences?
What if you are the scribe writing as
you journey learning of Oneness instead of differences?

What if you had, instead of instructions,
the instructor Himself as you take your journey?
What if I've been there all along, helping
you to remember as you regain your lost memory?"

I guess this does shed new light on the
subject and changes my whole prospective.
I see no need to fear the new growth
when it's so easy just to learn to be receptive.

I Sometimes Forget, but I Always Know

August 27, 1996

In the garden of life some
rows seem dry and much harder to hoe,
until I remember what I may
have forgotten, but will always know.

As I am traveling, I've
encountered a rough place in the road.
It's only temporary, It's not
forever, I can get over it, I've been told.

Just a few weeks ago, life
was so different, so filled with joy.
I was drunk on life. I was
like a kid and life was my new toy.

I remember that the rough places
are to help me grow and be stronger.
I know that I still have lessons
to learn and some take a little longer.

Doubt, confusion and fear seem to
have joined me on my journey for a while.
They make moving in the higher
direction a lot harder as I go another mile.

As I observe, I feel more afraid that
I'm giving the disorders of my ego my power.
I don't and won't consciously choose
to do this, or at least try not to for this hour.

I remember, in my soul, about
this journey I'm on and where I'm going.
I remember who I am, and
why I'm here. I remember through knowing.

I have to keep this knowledge and
my memories at the front of my mind.
Otherwise I would be swallowed up
in the pain and my soul would be in a bind.

God, through His grace, through
this gift of writing poems has taught me
that if I would remember to look past
the pain, His purpose for my life I would see.

To Him, little challenges of no
money for the bills is not a really big thing.
After all He owns the cattle on
a thousand hills and I'm a child of this King.

He makes a way where to
others there seems to not be one.
I, as His child, am to follow
His directions, as this race I run.

This is not easy when I feel weak, but He
reminds me that He's my strength for the day.
It's not easy when I feel so alone and afraid,
but He reminds me He's my courage for the way.

As I come upon a rough place in
the road, that makes my journey slow,
I'm reminded of what I may have
forgotten, but what I'll always know.

Extraordinary Things Happen When We Take a Vacation From the Ordinary

August 31, 1996

I wonder if we could change the ebb and
flow of life just by changing some old habits and such.
What if one morning, just out of the blue,
for no reason, instead of breakfast, we decided to have lunch?

What if, instead of sleeping to the
last minute and being awaken by the alarm,
we chose to not set the clock, but
woke up whenever! Who would that harm?

What if, instead of rushing around
and putting on our work or school disguise,

the family gathered together with
coffee and juice in hand and toasted the sunrise?

What if, instead of the same old daily
meeting human responsibilities and obligations,
the whole family played hooky and drove
to the country to observe God's other creations?

What if, instead of having a business
lunch talking about things that can't wait,
we spent a long lunch and whatever
with the one who we use to have time to date.

What if we dared to shift our perception
of the things that we see as important in our lives
to those beautiful gifts with which we are
entrusted, such as our children, husbands, and wives.

What if we dared to allow ourselves
the pure essence of joy and Thanksgiving,
by looking at life differently and
changing some of the things that aren't working.

What if, instead of being so bogged
down with the stresses of life's confrontations,
We saw life as one big happy party,
a time of loving and an on going celebration.

I wonder what extraordinary things we might
see in our lives just by veering from the ordinary?
It doesn't have to be any thing big, nothing
outlandish, just a shift from what is customary.

Words Seem So Inadequate

October 17, 1996

As the feelings of awe, love,
gratitude, praise, and thanksgiving
swell up within my heart for this
miraculous gift of life that I'm living,
I find words are inadequate.

How can I, in my limited five
sense humanness, even dare to try
to express the joy, peace, and
love that brings tears to my eyes,
when words seem so inadequate.

It's like trying somehow to
describe the hues and lines
of a beautiful rainbow
to someone who is blind,
and words seem so inadequate.

Or try to describe the sound
of the wind or the song of a bird
to someone who is deaf and
these lovely gifts have never heard.
Words seem so inadequate.

To the creator of these
miracles, these beautiful gifts,
I want to thank and
songs of praise I want to lift,
but words seem so inadequate.

I've heard that actions
speak much louder than words,
so then I get caught up in
doing so that my love can be heard,
because words seem so inadequate.

Then sometimes in my zeal,
I forget my reason for the doing
and I get so busy I forget to
take the time for my mind's renewing,
because words seem so inadequate.

Time gets away so quickly
and the day or the week has past
before I remember what's really
important and that which will last
all because words seem so inadequate.

As I again take the time to
be quiet and center my mind,
I feel such love, joy, and
peace from my creator so divine,
and words seem so inadequate.

How do I say thank you? How
do I express my gratitude and praise?
Could it be in the time spent in
loving communion as my voice I raise,
with words that seem so inadequate?

The Quietness of Waiting

November 26, 1996

On this journey of
life we are never alone.
God is closer to us
than our cellular phone.

He has blest us
with the gift of Grace.
It goes before us
as we run in life's race.

Grace makes the
crooked path straight
and is recognized
only by those who wait.

Waiting is the secret,
you know, of joy and peace.
For it is in the quietness
of waiting that strife will cease.

It's in the quietness of
waiting that we can go within
and it's there we commune
with God as friend to friend.

It's in this same beautiful
place of quietness and waiting
that we receive so many gifts
that are ours just for the taking.

It's in this quietness of
waiting that our strength is renewed,
it's then we mount up with wings
as eagles soaring with power endued.

We will walk and not be
weary and we will run and not faint.
We receive all this power and
strength as with God, we quietly wait.

Happy Birthday, Jesus

December 10, 1996

Jesus, we celebrate that wondrous
day, the miraculous gift of your birth.
The day God lovingly let you go,
and sent you to live here on this earth.

We can only imagine the joy of
those who in awe prepared to welcome you,
for they were blest to learn that
through you other miracles would come, too.

We want to celebrate the awesome
gift of our blessed spiritual birth as well.
For because of your guidance, we, with
child like faith, can choose heaven over hell.

With that same faith, we have
accepted our unique purpose for being.
We celebrate the miracles we've
experienced and in others we are now seeing.

We celebrate each day that because of
your Grace we can peacefully and joyfully live.
We celebrate that through us, to others,
your love and compassion you are able to give.

We celebrate that wondrous
day, the miraculous gift of your birth.
The day God, with love, knowing
you would return, sent you to live on earth.

Happy Birthday and Everyday

Our Love

January 18, 1997

This poem is dedicated to my best friend and father of my children, Jim.

How selfish is a love that
wants to hold on and deny,
to keep caged the soul
that yearns to be free to fly?

How selfish to not want to
share and give back to the universe,
that which was not really ours,
but just borrowed for temporary use?

How unselfish is a love
that lets the loved one go,
that frees the caged soul
so that to others it can flow?

How unselfish is it knowing that
we do the most good for others, apart
and yet at the same time we will
lovingly hold each other in our hearts?

We do this because of our
love for God and the human race.
We do this because it's our
purpose and this task we gladly face.

Together for thirty five years,
we lived the first part of our mission.
Together we lovingly raised our
five children, grateful for that position.

Sadly some must lose their loved one by abandonment or one
leaving the planet making their transition.
I'm thankful that because we listened to our soul and
followed our hearts we only had to change our positions.

Thank you for a love that isn't
possessive and doesn't fear letting go.
Thank you for the courage to
accept your freedom as to others you show

That one is not alone or
separated just because we live miles apart.
We have been joined for eternity
because we live in each other's hearts.

God Is So Cool

January 24, 1997

Oh, God, I think that you,
with all your wisdom, are so cool.
You allow us experiences
and challenges as a learning tool.

A tool for us to better
know and understand you
as first our mind and then
our life you teach us to renew.

We learn to search for wisdom as
we would search for a hidden treasure.
What we find is love and peace for
ourselves and others, more than we can measure.

Thank you, for the gift of finding God
the Good in our experiences, in earth's school.
Thank you, thank you for the joy of
being an expression of a God who is so cool.

The Miracle of a Changed Mind

January 31, 1997

It's only by the changing
or the renewing of our mind,
that we can courageously
move on leaving the past behind.

No longer is it necessary to be
victims only living with our fears.
Instead we are more than
conquerors of the illusion that appears.

It isn't our dysfunctional
childhood that is holding us back.
It's the choosing to remain
a victim carrying around our sack.

It's only when we begin to
remember who we are and why we are here
that we can drop the sack of
manure from the past and we no longer fear.

We don't fear what happened yesterday
or even of what tomorrow might bring.
It's learning to live today, in this moment
that gives us peace and makes our soul sing.

Now Is the Time

February 4, 1997

I'm sure that if we thought
about it, we don't really mean to.
I'm sure that it could be just
an unconscious thing that we do.

Instead of being free in us to
live, move, and have His Being,
we keep Him tucked away
nice and neat for our own seeing.

Maybe we're afraid that if we
share with the world what we know,
some might think us fanatical,
mad, or drunk from the wine's glow.

So we keep Him to ourselves
waiting and hoping that someone will ask
to know the secret of our peace,
joy, happiness and our love that lasts.

Inside, our soul wants so much to
share and to have the stone rolled away,
but instead we push it down,
maybe even forgetting until another day.

How very sad is this secret
game of life that we continue to play.
We are afraid to share because
of what others may do, think, or say.

I'm sure that if we would take the risk
to be courageous and say the first word
we would then hear from another,
and another until all have been heard.

We would then know that there are
others who are aware of their journey
who are being blest as grace carries
them, too, past the point of no returning.

So, you see, we are not alone, there are
others just like us with miracles unending.
Don't you think now is the time to sound the
trumpet and shout the message that He's sending?

Transformation

February 9, 1997

I sat thinking this morning about the butterfly
and how it would be a terrible state of affairs
if it, in its ignorance and fear, chose to remain
in its cocoon instead of experiencing the fresh air.

The Universe would indeed suffer a
great loss of beauty, grace, and regeneration
if the butterfly chose to stay safe in its
cocoon instead of completing its transformation.

Or, what if it, in its ignorance and fear,
chose to stay a caterpillar always hiding and destroying,
instead of choosing to complete its
transformation and all its beauty and grace be showing?

There is a lesson to be learned by
watching the butterfly in its different stages.
It's the same lesson we as humans
have been experiencing down through the ages.

We, too, develop and grow through different
experiences as we learn through the choices we make.
We arrived here as a babe all perfect and new and
we grew into the adult finding we've made mistakes.

We weave a safe cocoon around us through
the knowledge we gain as our Higher Self we seek.
Until the day comes when we break loose
from our shell for this Truth we can no longer keep.

The universe would indeed suffer a
great loss of beauty, grace, and regeneration
if we chose to stay safe in our comfort
zone instead of completing our transformation.

It's Important to Remember

February 11, 1997

It is not important
that I see the big picture,
it's more important
that I remember there is one.

It is not important that I
understand how the Universe works,
it's more important
that I remember that it does.

It is not important that I
know what the future holds,
it's more important that I
remember Who holds the future.

It is not important to be
concerned with the hereafter,
it's more important to remember
to be conscious of the now.

It is not important to
dwell on our pain or mistakes,
it's more important to remember
to learn and grow from them.

It is not important to
see something to believe it,
it's more important to remember
to believe and then we will see it.

It is not important to change
ourselves so that we can love ourselves,
it's more important to remember that it is because
we love ourselves that we want to make changes.

It is not important just
to see the glass as half full,
it's more important to remember that
we've already enjoyed the first half.

It is not important to live
for the praise of humanity,
it's more important to remember that we are
to live as the praise of God to humanity.

It is not important to try
to earn God's love by doing,
it's more important to remember that we
are already loved because of our Being.

It is not important how we
humans arrived here on the planet,
it's more important to remember
who we are and our purpose for Being.

It is not important that we be
remembered when we are gone,
it's more important that God be
remembered because we were here.

Section Three

My Wisdom: God's Gift To Me, My Gift To You

***Knowledge is bought with money —
Wisdom is bought with experience.***

Writing As A Metaphor

I feel that writing this book has been a metaphor of living my life. There were times, in my human thinking, that I thought it would be much simpler if God gave "it" to me "right" the first time instead of me having to spend so much time going over parts of it seemingly thousands of times editing, changing, adding to, and deleting. Sometimes it was something small like a comma here and there and sometimes it was bigger like a whole page.

Now that it's finished, I wouldn't change the way He did it, for I found that most every time I went back over a section I would receive something new or I would be reminded of something that I had forgotten.

I'm sure the writing still won't be perfect in the eyes of some, but I'm okay with that. There will be punctuation marks out of place or maybe a dangling something or other here and there, it's okay. One of the lessons I needed to learn was to not be so concerned with perfect appearances. In my life I have experienced lots of changes, some little and some huge. I have edited a lot of old stuff that I no longer needed that was keeping me in bondage. At the same time so much has been added to make my living a joyous peaceful experience.

I probably broke the first rule in writing right from the start because I didn't use an outline. I would jot down fragments of thoughts and insights and then, like at one thirty this morning, I would awaken and everything fit together like a puzzle. If I had a couple of paragraphs that didn't feel right, I knew eventually I would receive what I needed to make them fit.

Though my life didn't come with instructions, I received insights and knowledge along the way. Sometimes I might not understand what I was receiving from the challenges and experiences, but one day it would hit me and I understood. When I became aware of the importance of looking for the Good (or God) in all things, my understanding became more clear and my life became more joyous and peaceful.

Some of the writing has been physically painful because of arthritis and because of an injured index finger on my right hand, I had to wear a splint for a few weeks. Some of my living has been very emotionally painful. Some because of the self imposed splints that I put on my feelings to keep them immobile. Again, this was bondage.

Sometimes I would think I was almost finished and then I would have a writing spurt and I would learn more. Sometimes I thought I had had all the pain and learning experiences that I could stand and about the time I was ready to call it quits, I found joy and peace from within.

Sometimes I would feel impatient because getting the book finished and making sure it was right (perfect) was taking much to long. Yet, I savored every minute, because this writing, this allowing Spirit to speak through me, like all other ways of being creative, is as close to God as a human can get. Yet, we can only receive these creative gifts as we allow ourselves to be close to God. It's when we are a part of a creation, or of creating, that we know God and feel the Oneness with all creation.

Sometimes I get impatient with life. I am not sure I am doing things right. I fear that I may be a hindrance some way to God living through me. Then when I'm talking to Him about it, He takes me to a higher place and shows me that when He is living through me, I'm perfect. I'm where I'm supposed to be, doing what I'm supposed to be doing. And what I'm doing is being that expression of God.

Sometimes I felt so much joy, love, and awe when I received a poem or when new thoughts, or a new understanding of old ones, flashed across my mind that I wanted to yell it from the mountain top, send it in a letter to someone, or just share with anyone that would listen. It was like falling in love. I felt like I was going to burst if I didn't share these miracles with someone. This gave me more reason to get this book finished and on the shelves for those who are waiting for it. I knew all along that the truth found in these pages were for me first, to heal me so I could help others on their journey with their healing. Because of the knowledge that I have received, life has become a celebration of miracles. I'm drunk on life and don't EVER want to be sober again.

There were times that were very painful to my soul because I had this longing, this desire that came from deep within my soul to share, then when I tried to share, I was refused or rejected. I had all this love, all these miracles swelling up inside that I wanted to share and I found that there were people who weren't interested. I saw this as a metaphor of humanity's relationship with God.

I was even asked what made me think anyone would be interested in reading my book and hearing my story. I was told that the world really didn't need another book. Just look at all the ones out there. It was suggested that because people didn't buy factual books as much, maybe I should consider writing it as fiction so I could reach a larger audience. Another loving soul suggested that I might want to just publish Section One and Two, only because Section Three was so "preachy."

Though painful, this was a beautiful learning experience for it created a lot of self doubt and fear for me to learn to overcome. It challenged what I believed and knew within my soul as Truth. I could have so easily given up on the book and on life. Yet I remembered that all I had to do was change my thinking so I learned to accept and work through my feelings. I learned to depend on my Higher Self, this Spirit within, which was the reason for my searching for and finding my Self. I had to believe in my Self whether anyone else did or not. I had to shift the looking at experiences with my human eyes and look at them through the eyes of my loving Higher Self, who only sees love and Goodness. I had to remember who I was and the reason for my being here. I had to remember that I had invited God to live, move and have His Being in and through me. I had to remember that I lived, moved and had my Being in Him. I had to remember that I had volunteered a long time ago to come to this planet and be an expression and a manifestation of God. I had to remember that though I chose this human form and though I had to deal with the ego part of myself, I was a Spiritual Being with only one purpose as that expression of God, and that was to Love and to see everyone and everything as the same expression of God's love as I am.

At the same time, with my human understanding I could see God, or the Higher Self in each one of us trying to share more Love and more Good with us and in our ignorance and fear, we refused or rejected it. I could see God, or our Higher Self wanting so much for us to remember who we are, where we came from, why we are here, and where we were to return, yet we weren't ready to listen, or to learn so that we could remember. Our higher Self wanted so much to help us find within ourselves peace, joy, and an everlasting Love, but we refused.

Sometimes, because of ignorance and fear, we think we already know it all. After all we have been in church thirty, forty, or fifty years. God is the same yesterday, today, and forever so there is nothing new to learn. We know everything ABOUT God that we need to know. We certainly don't want to listen to or accept any new thoughts or anything that is different than the "old time religion" that has been passed down from generation to generation. So we stay bound and won't allow ourselves to be free "in the Spirit" to KNOW GOD at a higher level of consciousness.

I'm afraid, in my human thinking and with my impatience, I would have said, "to hell with the whole bunch of you. If you choose to be to busy or too ignorant to search for me, then why should I care if you accept my gifts or not."

I am so thankful that in God's grace, He is so patient, loving and understanding. He knows that one day we will remember.

Yes, writing my Spiritual autobiography, just like my life, has been a learning or a relearning experience to help me to remember who I am, where I came from, what my purpose is and to where I'm returning. Remembering is like my being reunited with my loved ones from whom I had been separated for forty eight years. Though I can't remember what happened with them as that baby, by listening to their stories, I can learn. Then we began to make new memories as a family of adults. Because we were reunited, we know that even though we had been separated for all those years by miles and time, we had still been family. We had still been brother and sisters and we always will be. The same blood flows through each one of us. That knowledge can never be taken away.

To learn that through my family, this was a real life metaphor for learning about my spiritual relationship, I had to be willing for Spirit to move me beyond the self made boundaries and limitation of this five sense human to a higher level. I had to experience the quietness and stillness with meditation. I read like someone starving and I wrote like someone filled to overflowing. I invited Spirit or my Higher Self to make It's Self known to me. I learned to look for God in every person, in every thing, in every experience, in every challenge, and in every circumstance. I wanted to see God the Good, the God of Love in all people and in all things, for I knew He was there.

Transformation

"And do not be conformed to this world, but be transformed by the renewing of your mind, that you may prove what is that

good and acceptable and perfect will of God." Romans 12:2

Unlike Brother Paul, most of us don't have a "Damascus Road Experience." Instead we are here just trying to "do" what is right in the sight of God and man. A day will come, however, when because of some kind of pain and/or suffering, our wounded soul cries out and then we move to the next stage of our transformation. This is our conscious journey of relearning or remembering who we are and why we are here.

At first some of us may try to find healing for our life, by conforming our beliefs and thoughts to the world of pain and suffering, as we have come to know it. We do this religiously by using the same laws, rules, traditions, ideas, and beliefs that everyone before us did. We end up with the same result as everyone before us did. Whether it works or not, this is all passed from one generation to another.

It doesn't have to be that way anymore. We, and thus our circumstances, can be transformed or changed by renewing our minds first. The first step in renewing our minds is choosing to accept the fact, that for what ever reason; be it our past, our parents, our lack of knowledge, our fears, or where ever else we want to place the blame, we are in a mess and are thus experiencing hell. Next, after we admit that we are absolutely powerless over what happened to us and the effects that it has had on us, we choose to turn it over to our Higher Power. We then choose to believe that He is in us waiting for us to ask for His wisdom and then we can learn to listen to His small voice inside. I use to wonder why He used a quiet voice instead of knocking us over the head or yelling. I think it's because He wants us to be quiet, to stop ranting and raving about how bad the world is, how bad our life is, how terrible people are, etc. We have to be quiet or we will miss hearing Him. When we do listen, then others can see the changes which proves that changes can take place. By our sharing, others can make the same discoveries in their own life and so on, and so on, and so on.

Even though I gave my heart to God when I was eight years old and have tried to live for Him as best as humanly possible, I have found that there is more to Spirituality than making a profession of faith, being baptized, going to church, Temple, Synagogue, or Mass, reading my Bible, counting beads, lighting candles, praying, and trying to obey and live under the old laws, the traditions, rituals, and ceremonies. All of these are good and necessary for our spiritual growth. However, as Brother Paul wrote in Romans chapters 5-8, it is impossible in our humanness to always "do it right." Because of our many failures and short comings, some choose to give up and say, "what's the use?"

Though I have been exposed to, I have not been a student of religions or philosophies. I grew up as a child and lived as an adult in the Judeo-Christian faith. While this faith helped me to get to this stage of my transformation, what I share with you today comes straight from the Source through my personal experiences. Mom West always told me that a bought lesson was better than a borrowed one.

There is a Higher level of Spiritual consciousness that goes beyond our five senses. This is the Higher Self for which I had been searching. This is not something that one just learns or knows ABOUT. It is something that has to be experienced. I believe that Dr. Peale experienced it. The Fillmores and Joel Goldsmith experienced it. Wayne Dyer, Depak Chopra, M.S. Peck, and many others are experiencing it.

It was with this knowledge that I, like the caterpillar, could go within to this Higher Consciousness, the larva or cocoon, and my transformation could continue. It was there that old thoughts and beliefs could be changed or looked at in a different light.

It was there that I could learn to see my experiences, both past and present, from a different prospective. Because of God's grace going before me making the crooked places straight,

I learned that all I had to do was stay out of the way. I began to see the experiences of life as opportunities for miracles because I learned that He has a perfect plan for my life. Everything that I would ever need is already mine. Everything happens in Divine order not only for my good, but for His good pleasure and for His delight.

I learned that I was One with Him. I lived, moved, and had my Being in Him and at the same time, He lived, moved, and had His Being in me. All I had to do was transform my thinking just a little. It was then that I found that all I had to do was to believe and then I could see.

It was then that I could fully trust Him in every area of my life. Because of the gift of Free Will in every choice that I make, I have the authority to ask for His guidance. I can then detach from any outcome for I know whatever happens is for the "GOOD."

If I forget to ask for guidance and I judge that I made a mistake, I can make repairs, forgive myself and accept it as yet another learning experience, thus letting it go and not dwelling on it.

This transformation brings with it the freedom and the responsibility to just "Be" that beautiful butterfly expressing and manifesting God in all His Glory.

While it is true that everyday spirituality is not an escape from our usual life in search of some special "experience," it is not the bringing spirituality "down" to the human level (living Romans 5-8), but rather lifting our humanness to a higher spiritual consciousness. It is only by the transforming or changing our human ego centered thoughts into the higher God consciousness that we are able to surrender into the fullness of every experience. Only then can we see the spiritual within the ordinary and everyday challenges and experiences. Only then can we look at any situation, event, circumstance, or person and choose to see the Good. Only then can we live peacefully and lovingly in the now.

The Divine order of our transformation does not happen over night. It's a process similar to that of the butterfly evolving from the egg to the caterpillar, to the Pupa inside a cocoon, and then into the magnificent creation that we see dance so beautifully free in the breeze. The result of our transformation is no less beautiful and no less freeing.

We, in our ignorance, are like the caterpillar in the egg. We know of nothing except being confined in the darkness and being alone. In the Divine order of things we break through the shell and find ourselves surrounded by light. This is when we first experience salvation.

We find that we can crawl around going from leaf to leaf and plant to plant. This is such freedom compared to what we just evolved from. We may be so happy in this stage that we never think that there are other stages with even more freedom and so much more beauty. We may find there are other life forms (or ideas) many of which are different from us. We may judge them unfairly instead of just accepting them as they are. Because of fear and ignorance, we may even go so far as to try to destroy them.

Some people believe, like I did, that any further stages of transformation happens only after we die and go to heaven. Some people, by choice, live and die as the caterpillar not being aware of the next two stages and the complete transformation.

In the Divine order of things, we hear or read something that ignites a spark in our soul. We then come to the stage where we choose to ignore or we choose to answer our soul's cry to know a Higher Self. It's then that we learn to go inside (the cocoon) and seek guidance from a higher state of consciousness. It is then that we consciously choose to seek for knowledge to renew our mind and change our old limited thinking.

Unlike the butterfly, our transformation is not a one time event. Every time that we choose to change our mind and see a situation or a challenge in a loving positive way, we have made a transformation.

It is only through these stages (of awareness) that we can "prove what is that good and acceptable and perfect will of God." It is only then that we can evolve or transform into the beautiful graceful, regenerating Being that we were meant to be. It is then that we will remember who we are and we can carry out the purpose for which we are here on the planet.

Tuesday, May 28, 1996, 4:45 am

Today I am thinking about the Divine order of events that enabled my life's transformations during the past almost four years:

1.) June 23, 1992, following the annual Brown Family Reunion, I was fed up with life as I knew it. I was feeling unloved, insecure, and unhappy (wake up call). Made the call to Kaiser Mental Health and talked to Dr. K. for the first time. (This was not an office visit as my records states, but a telephone call about three in the afternoon. The first office visit was about three weeks later because I remember thinking, "I don't know if I can hang on for three weeks.")

2.) October 1992 joined SIA support group. Being a twelve step support group, I was reminded of the power I had within. I learned to ask God for the serenity to accept the things that I couldn't change and to ask for the courage to change the things I could, and the wisdom to know the difference. This was but an expansion of the knowledge I already had, but wasn't practicing or enjoying to the fullest extent. Working with this group gave me the opportunity to both give and receive. They became my spiritual family.

3.) February 1993 was journaling prolificly and had started receiving the gift of poems. I knew that I was to share the story of my journey with others in a book.

4.) October 1993 had more pain than I could handle. Asked God for help. Listening to the quiet voice inside I learned to ask for and even fight for what I truly believed I needed. The first step to growing up and taking responsibility, with God's guidance, for my life.

5.) February 27, 1994, after spending a tremendous amount of energy in preparation for committing suicide in April, I had a dream and received a poem (*Death's Arms*) about my purpose for being on this planet thus changing my mind about the suicide. Funny how my circumstances hadn't changed. All the pain was still there. Yet, my mind was changed.

6.) March 17, 1994, God increased my faith in Him and the belief in miracles by restoring contact with my birth siblings after forty eight years.

7.) April 6, 1994, Dr. K. suggested reading The Road Less Traveled, by M.S. Peck. Reading this book was a validation not only that my writing was coming from God, but also that I was right where I was supposed to be on my journey. When the librarian placed the book in my hand, I felt I was holding something Holy. I read his chapter on Spirituality first because that was what I had most recently been writing about. There it was in black and white some of the same things I had been writing, including some of the same scripture verses. We were saying the same thing tho mine may have come packaged a little differently.

8.) June 1994, Feeling depressed, but remembering I had a purpose and the miracles God was performing, I requested medical help for an antidepressant to help me get through the rough part of that time in my life, believing I would only be on it for short term. At that visit the doctor said that because of my "dependent, borderline, and histrionic" personality disorders, I would more than likely have to be on prozac for the rest of my life. I left there with my prozac in hand feeling like a whipped puppy. I felt that I had been sentenced to a life of victimhood with the effects of not one but three personality disorders, which according to the psychology books I read later, were irreversible because of my history. During that summer a war was going on within my soul creating a lot of confusion and unrest. I didn't know what it was until one night in my group therapy one of the ladies, who shared her same pathetic story week after week was feeling worse than usual. She was seeing a psychotherapist and was having a hard time getting all of her antidepressants to work together. She said he had told her that week that she would always be on medication and would never get better. Seeing the pain she was in, the hopelessness and helplessness in her voice, I flew into a rage, "How dare him play God with your life. You don't have to lay there and take that. You have power. You can fight. You don't have to believe him." I was shaking as the words spilled from my mouth. I felt sick at my stomach. It wasn't until later as I was journaling that I realized those words were for me. God was reminding me of the power I had residing within me. By seeking knowledge to learn to change my mind (which is not done over night) I had the power to reverse the irreversible.

9.) November 1994, I started working with Lisa individually on the issues of losses. I was able to do the grief work that I as an infant could not do. At the same time, Lisa became like a Spiritual Guide. It was during this time that the Grace of

God was indeed going before me. Not being familiar with the new knowledge that I was receiving, some of it contradicting old beliefs, I had opportunities to face challenges of self doubt and fear. I learned that it was okay to be different; to see and feel things differently; and to express them. Ended therapy March 14, 1995 with no separation anxiety.

10.) May, 1995, I started seeing DiannaLynn, who was Lisa's supervisor. She would not allow me to remain in the helpless, child like victim role; At the same time I started listening to Dr. Laura, when I could, after accidentally catching one of her programs on the radio; and I read the book, Beyond Victimhood, by Tom Fitzgerald, which was one of those books that fell into my hands at the bookstore. God was giving me the knowledge I asked for.

11.) August, 1995, Received opportunities to practice what I had been learning. A chance to practice and thus build more faith. Again, the pain was more than I could bear on my own. Again, I didn't remember to ask God for help first. I came closer to killing myself than I had in the past, even to taking a hand full of pills. However, when it was all over I learned that God was the only one in my life I could have confidence in. I learned He was the only faithful one. He was the only one I could trust. Even the prozac didn't have the power to save me from the effects of depression.

12.) October, 1995, In one of my therapy sessions with DiannaLynn, I was blasted over the hump that had kept me bound in my victim role. For the first time my body, soul and spirit became one. I realized my wholeness and at the same time my oneness with God. My body, soul and spirit were made totally free. I am no longer bound by the illusion of any power, including personality disorders, that would keep me from enjoying all the Good that God has for me. This is my salvation. I no longer have to endure hell. I no longer have a need for prozac. I terminated "on going therapy" realizing I have the Master Therapist living within me.

13.) March 1996, went on a Vision Quest into the desert. I had a life changing spiritual experience while watching a phenomenal sunrise. I saw with my eyes and heard with my ears God's heartbeat. I was aware that our hearts were beating simultaneously. It was there that I received the vision/dream of creating "Miracle Creations."

Their Theories

Ever since the human species became aware of their evolution, we have experienced "wake up" calls which lead us to search for answers to such questions as:

Who am I? What am I doing here? How did I get here? What is the meaning of life? Is this all there is to life? Is there really a God? What part is God supposed to play in my life? What does He expect of me? What can I expect of Him? How can I be happy?

We have used science, myths, philosophy, psychology, and religion to try to find the answers. Some even seek answers from traditions, ceremonies, rituals, body movements, and going to places that are said to be holy or sacred so they can communicate with A Higher Source, whatever their understanding of the Source might be, depending on what part of the universe they find themselves. The important thing to remember is that there are those who are actively seeking and searching for the answers for themselves and this is good.

We have the accounts in Genesis, known as the "creation story," which most of us have taken literally, but if one takes the time to go to the original writings and searches for themselves, learns that it is a myth or a story that someone wrote, with inspiration, with the knowledge they had, to try to give us an explanation of our "beginnings."

There is a theory held by some that we come to this planet for the purpose of healing old soul wounds or our personality. They believe that we may come hundreds and hundreds of times beginning with the form of a minute organism until we evolve into and take on the form of a human. They believe that we come, to learn whatever we need to learn to heal our souls as our spiritual part matures and we recognize who we are, a Spiritual Being. They believe that we will experience every form until we reach the highest form of Spirituality, meaning we have to think beyond our five senses. They believe that every time we come back we bring with us the knowledge that we have learned from previous lifetimes as well as the old wounds that we still need to have healed as well as the lessons that we still need to learn.

At the moment I'm reading two books. One is *The Soul's Code*, by James Hillman. In it he shares his "acorn" theory and the other one is, *A Parenthesis in Eternity*, by Joel Goldsmith. When Joel wrote this book in the early sixties he said it was about one hundred years before it's time. In *The Celestine Prophecy* and *The Tenth Insight*, James Redfield shares his theory. M.S. Peck shares his insights or theory in *The Road Less Traveled*, *Farther Along the Road Less Traveled* and his newest one, *The Road Less Traveled and Beyond*. Marianne Williamson shares her insights in, *A Return to Love*.

A lovely lady who is a resident of the nursing home where I read poetry, gave me a beautiful book titled, *The Family Album*, published by The Family Album in Valley Forge, Pa. In it I found a charming poem by Grace E. Easley, that expressed her theory in such a picturesque way:

God's Magnificence

We are explorers more or less,
In life's uncharted wilderness,
So much remains for those to find,
Who have an open, eager mind.
A miracle beyond belief,
The fragile texture of a leaf—
No laboratory can produce
A snow-capped mountain green with spruce.
No chemist's beaker can contain
The crystal formula of rain,
You will not find a patent on
The coral ribbons of the dawn.
Say what you will, nobody knows
What truly makes a living rose,
In spite of all we've learned so far,
Man cannot duplicate a star!

The cool gray moss, the ivied vine,
Aren't rolled from an assembly line,
The palette of the artist holds
No match for autumn's reds and golds.
The greatest sonnet ever penned,
Is but an echo of the wind—
And all things past and all things hence,
...Attest to God's Magnificence!

We have a wealth of information available to us, but how many of us use it? Eventually if we search long enough, we will learn that the information we need is available from within our own selves. We have the Source within us.

My Theory

"But we have renounced the hidden things of shame, not walking in craftiness nor handling the word of God deceitfully, but by manifestation of the truth commending ourselves to every man's conscience in the sight of God." 2nd Corinthians 4:2

I feel that because my secrets, which produced shame, are no longer hidden, I no longer have to walk around wearing my false mask. Because of the freedom that I'm now experiencing, I can, with confidence, share my feelings and opinions about anything I choose, even the taboo spiritual things that may be different from what I was taught. I understand that God gave us a conscience to decide what we choose to do with the information. In the sight of God I feel I'm doing what He wants me to do with the information I have.

In my own personal search, I have received enough knowledge only to have learned that the more I learn, the more I need to learn. There is a higher spiritual realm that I am striving for as I practice the presence of God. It seems by the many books on the market that God is trying to get our attention, to get us to think, to search, to discover Him, or our Higher Self. He wants us to know there is much more to life than what we have been taught. It is time for us to do our own research instead of relying just on the knowledge of others. The teachings we received in the past, the books, workshops, seminars, and classes are all here to kindle a spark in our soul, to get us to think, and to ask God for our own insights, to know Him in a more personal and intimate way.

If anyone has ever taken the time to think or even dared to question for themselves, they have seen so many seemingly contradictions in the Bible. Most of us don't get very far with this because we are reminded that these questions are coming from satan to confuse us. For heaven's sake don't think for yourselves because you might be confused and we have all learned that confusion is from satan.

I grew up and spent most of my adult life involved in good "fundamental" churches. (I only recently looked up the word fundamental to see what it meant.) The truth that I received there was just what I needed for that time in my life. It was, as the name implies, fundamental for my spiritual growth and awareness.

However, there comes a time in our life when our soul yearns for more. This is when we receive our "wake up" calls. This is when our transformation moves us along to the next stage of our spiritual growth and awareness. This is when the healing from our Spiritual amnesia becomes more aggressive.

Again, it's our choice if we want to answer our wake up calls or if we want to stay asleep a little longer. It's our choice because of our spiritual lethargicness to remain in our ignorance and fear or, if we want, we can wake up and start remembering who wc arc and our purpose for being here on this planet.

This is my theory and insights that I have gleaned from my personal research. I believe that our purpose for being here on this planet is very simple. God created the plant, mineral, and animal life for us to take care of and love. We did not come to this planet to "be in our own little world" and look out just for ourselves. We are here to love and care for each other because we are all connected. I've learned that when I am loving and kind towards another, I am even more blest than they. I believe we are here as gifts to each other. Part of our mission may be to provide challenges and learning experiences for those around us in our everyday life just like there are those who are here to do the same for us. As hard as it might be to believe, one day we will thank them for our learning experiences. In my own experience some of my teachers have already left the planet, but I believe they know that I have forgiven them and I thank them.

I believe that we are here to be an expression or manifestation of God. I believe that He has given us Grace and Mercy to go before us making the crooked places straight. (We only need to stay out of the way). I believe that we are His hands, eyes, ears, feet, and heart. Because we are made in His likeness or His image, which is Divine Love, our purpose or mission as that expression or manifestation of God is to Love, not in a human selfish way, but in God's unselfish and unconditional way. No matter what our, race, creed, profession, sexual preference, religion, education, past, or what's happening in our life at this moment; whether we choose to live under the law or under Grace, whether we believe that we only get one time here on this planet or if we believe that we may visit here thousands of times, it just doesn't matter. We all have the same purpose, the same task, the same mission and that is to Love every thing, including circumstances, challenges and experiences. We are to Love everything from the smallest annoying insects, animals, trees, oceans, and sky; we are to Love everyone regardless of race, creed, sexual preference, and religion; we are to Love every person, place, and thing; animal, plant or mineral, not just on this planet, but in the whole Universe. All of these are creations, expressions, and manifestations of God, just like us and they came with the same mission, to Love. We are one with all of these, regardless of what kind of form that we or they chose to come to this planet as; regardless of race, creed, sexual preference, or religion.

We don't remember any of this because we are suffering from a dis-ease called Spiritual Amnesia. However, I believe at this very moment we are being healed of our Spiritual Amnesia and when we remember these things we will accept and Love everyone and everything unconditionally. It's that simple. We'll spend more time on this subject later.

Just think about it, when we hold a brand new baby, we are holding pure unadulterated innocent unconditional Divine

Love. We are holding the pure Essence of God. We have no problem Loving this helpless dependent little Being with unconditional Love. Even when it spits up on us just as we are running out the door; or when it awakens us in the middle of the night; or when it demands our attention when we are in the middle of something we feel important; even when we are experiencing those postpartum blues, we still can't help but to Love. It's as if this little Being has a magnet within that draws Love from us and at the same time it is giving so freely without even doing anything except being.

There is a good illustration in one of the *Chicken Soup for the Soul*, books about a little boy who asked to spend a few minutes alone with his new baby sibling. The parents felt a little apprehensive, but agreed. They had a monitor on in the room and they heard the little boy say, "please tell me about God because I think I am about to forget."

Yes, we knew how to Love and receive Love when we first came to this planet, but because of different challenges and experiences (brain washing) while growing up, which created wounds to our souls, we learned to be fearful; because of getting so entangled with the things of the world, we unconsciously developed ambivalence toward spiritual things; and because these things caused abuse to our spirituality, we developed the dis-ease, Spiritual Amnesia. Because of this dis-ease, we have forgotten who we are, where we came from, what our purpose for being here is, and about our destination. Instead of using our spiritual instinct, we developed human instinct which comes from our ego. Everything that is Good and perfect that comes from the Love of God, the ego creates the opposite because of fear. This is the result of the wonderful gift of "free will" that God gave us.

I think of the feral children who were raised by wolves. Whether they are real or a myth, I don't know, but I find the idea to be a great metaphor about us as Spiritual Beings coming here and taking on the less than perfect behaviors of humans. When they were found, even though they were human, because they were raised as animals; because of their environment; because they had forgotten who they really were; they took on the behaviors of the animals. However, they were still in human bodies.

I enjoy the movie, Hook. Little Maggie had several lines that reminded me of our journey here. To me, Captain Hook and all his buddies (the grown ups) remind me of our thoughts produced from our ego or human consciousness. When Captain Hook was trying to brainwash Jack and Maggie telling them that their parents didn't love them, I was reminded of all the brainwashing and lies that we encounter in our daily lives that try to get us to not only forget about our Father/Mother God, but to forget who we are. I remember the times that I couldn't believe that God could love me because I thought I was such a bad person.

One line that Maggie said to Jack as she was being taken away after her brainwashing class was, "Remember, Jack, remember and run home."

At another time when her father was fighting Captain Hook she said, "Let's just go home, he's just a mean old man who didn't have a mother."

Don't you think that is the way with the people that we judge as bad. They just don't remember their Father/Mother God. Maybe if we could just focus our energy on who we are and on our going home.....

Our life today is not for practice. This is not a dress rehearsal for heaven. This is it, here and now. When we receive our "wake up call" we have been given the opportunity to choose to receive knowledge and make our living here on this planet better or roll back over and go back to sleep. Which ever we choose it's perfectly all right because we will receive another "wake up call" and another, and another, and another, until one day we will make a wiser choice. We have the Power, at this moment, living within us to make our life either heaven or hell. It is our choice. It is up to us.

It's only when we truly know who we are and that we are Loved with God's unconditional Love, that we will be open to even trying to understand, accept, and feel compassion for the whole Universe. It's only when we choose to see everyone else as that same expression and manifestation of God with the same potentiality, as we, to be healed of their Spiritual Amnesia that we will see Peace on earth. It's only then that we will no longer feel the fear that drives us, whether consciously or unconsciously to want to exert external power to hurt, manipulate, control, ridicule, judge or try to change another person. It's when we learn to accept the reality that everyone is on their own Spiritual path, experiencing their own Spiritual evolution at this precise moment, using the knowledge that they have, just like you and me, that we can experience Peace. Peace does not come from anything external or from any human endeavor. Peace comes from recognizing the internal Power that we have in us and it is that part of us which we are expressing as we Love. Yes, even the murderers, rapist, child molester, child abuser, thieves, liars, cheaters, those who are judgmental, rude, and unloving are all on their paths and come across our paths to teach us to love unconditionally as God loves. When we can remember that everyone in the Universe has the same mission or task and that some of us have different ways in which we are to manifest or express God's Love, then we can find Peace. Some souls, with compassion and love, have volunteered to come here just to get in our face so we can have the opportunity to remember how to Love and practive Forgiveness. When we truly learn to be the expression or manifestation of God by allowing Him to Love unconditionally through us, there will no longer be a need for such experiences, challenges, or people in our lives to teach us. There will no longer be a need for forgiveness. There will no longer be a need for fear. There will only be expressions and manifestations of God. There will only be Love. Then will all animal and human instincts cease and only the Loving instinct of Spirit will reign. Then will the lion lay down with the lamb because Love is the absence of fear. Then will we all know of our Oneness and then we will know Peace. I found that Isaiah 11:1-9 has a lot to say about the importance of this knowledge.

Loving someone with God's unconditional love is not saying, "I love their soul or the spirit in them, but they are wrong, they are rude, they are evil, they don't deserve to live. Unless they live the way I think they should they are going to hell. I don't want them living on my street, I don't want them going to my kid's school, I don't want them going to my church if they are going to wear those clothes or if their hair is that long or that color. I don't want them attending my church if they are gay or if they believe differently than I. I don't want them speaking at my Christian ladies luncheon if they go to that church or believe that way."

By the way, I have read and heard that these people who are such challenges for us are mirroring our real self. Because we don't have eyes on the inside of us, we can't see the wounds that are there. These helpful souls are showing us what we really look like. They are showing us that part of ourselves that we are expressing in our daily lives. They are showing us the human part of ourselves known as the ego. They are showing us and giving us a chance to see what we might want to forgive or change within. They are showing us what we may want to forgive in someone else in our past.

Maybe we need to see these things first in ourselves so we can learn to Love ourselves just as we are. It is easy to Love the spirit within ourselves and others, but it is hard, with our human understanding, to Love the ego or human part of us because all we see are imperfections. That's why we want to learn to look past the human or ego part and behold the Christ in each other. It is impossible to recognize and see the Christ in others if we don't first recognize and see the Christ as our Self. It is hard to give Love to another unless we have that Love for our Self. How can we give to another that which we don't posses. I can't give you oranges if all I have is apples.

Fear and ignorance are two challenges which are manifestations and expressions of our ego. They try to hinder us from our fulfilling our tasks or missions. Fear begets the feeling of powerlessness and powerlessness begets more fear. Our ignorance creates fear. What we fear, we hate and what we hate we want to destroy. We have to stop this vicious circle if we are to experience Peace.

Maybe if we could see our, as well as everyone else's ego, as a hungry wounded animal in need of comfort, food, and Love, but because of fear it chooses to attack instead of accepting what our spirit within wants to give, then maybe we can have some understanding and compassion not only for ourselves, but for the rest of humanity. Maybe then we can start to accept our ego part, Loving it, and thanking it for all the lessons or challenges that it sends our way to help us remember who we are and why we are here. Maybe when we can learn to accept our mistakes as painful learning experiences, which we have chosen to help us experience our good, then maybe we can understand the scriptures, "*All things are of God*" and "*All things work to the Good to them who love the Lord and are called according to His purpose*," (which is to be a manifestation and expression of God Himself). He called us and we volunteered to come here to this planet to Love. When we can remember this, then we will have learned the first step in learning to Love ourselves, which is the first step in learning to accept and Love others.

God's Grace plays an important part in our journey. There will always be someone in our lives who we see and can make the statement, "Except for the Grace of God that could be me." I'm wondering if we could look past their actions, remembering that Christ dwells within them, but they don't remember it and they are reacting from fear caused by their wounded souls. Could we treat them differently. If we were that person how would we want to be treated?

I was awaken three times the other night with the Golden Rule on my mind. I had always thought of it as, if I wanted to be treated kindly, I needed to treat others kindly. What I saw the other night was that no matter how we treat others, kind or unkind, that will be the treatment we will receive. It's just a Spiritual law. What you give out, whether it's money, love, time, judgment, unkindness, what ever, that, is what you will receive back.

Since most of us have heard and thus believed that we are unworthy wretched sinners going straight to hell if we didn't do life perfectly, it has been hard to Love our Self. Since we judge others by our own expectation, how can we Love them?

Most of us were raised with the idea that we are to Love God first, others second, and then ourselves. That isn't what Jesus taught. He left with us only two commandments. One is to Love the Lord our God with all our heart and the other is to Love everyone else as we Love our Self. Only when we can behold the Christ as our Self and behold Him in others can we fulfill these commandments.

In recovery this was illustrated by the metaphor of the oxygen mask on the airplane. If an emergency arises where it is necessary to use one of the masks and if there are children, for most of us our instincts would have us to put the masks on the children first. However, we are instructed to do the opposite and to put our mask on first so that we will be able to have enough oxygen to help the children with theirs.

I believe that there are two differences between Jesus Christ's mission and our mission here on the planet. One is that before He was conceived, an angel appeared to His Mom telling her what a Holy thing she was about to do as her expression and manifestation of God's Love, by bringing into the world this precious miracle. She was told that He would have the task or mission of being the expression and manifestation of God while He journeyed here on the planet. He would be here to Love others and teach them by His words and actions how to Love.

Can you imagine the impact of the spiritual healing on this planet if, before a woman conceived, an angel appeared to her and told her all about the precious miracle she was going to be having grow inside of her. What if she was told that this little Being would have the mission or task to be an expression or manifestation of God and was sent here to Love and be a way show-er? What if she was told that she was to help this little Being remember by expressing God's Love to it and everything around? She was to allow this precious miracle to express and remind others while growing up. What do you think would be changed or done differently about the way we raised these precious gifts from God? How do you think we would look at our Self differently if we were aware of this mission of allowing this Precious Being to grow inside of us?

(Scribe's note: As I was writing those words, I thought to my Self how great it would be if when we were expecting a baby, or if we had the joy of being caretakers of children, we had some information concerning what their personality would be like or any special instructions that would help us in caring for their soul. It would be so good to have something to remind us of the pure potentiality that we had entrusted in our hands to help mold. A few weeks later I was introduced to two books which are as close to what I had asked for as we could get. One is titled, *Sun Signs*, by Linda Goodman and the other is titled, *The Life You Were Born To Live*, by Dan Millman.)

If we would stop and remember, Jesus' natural family was somewhat dysfunctional. After all, His Mother was pregnant before she was married so more than likely He was looked upon as illegitimate. During those times that was a hard fact to have to overcome because you were like an outcast In His humanness He could have developed a poor self image. As an adult He could have considered Himself a victim of His past and blamed his parents for any challenges that came His way. He could have gotten all caught up in His victimhood, given in to ignorance and fear, and forgot all about the mission He came here to do.

However, thank God, just like He arose from the grave that had Him bound, He rose above His past because He remembered who He was. He remembered His purpose. He remembered His mission.

I'm wondering if because of the knowledge that His Mom had, maybe she was constantly reminding Him of His purpose for being here on the planet. I'm sure that He was in constant communication with God which was just as natural to Him as getting a drink of water when He was thirsty. He never forgot who He was, where He came from, why He was here, and where His destination was when He finished. He had no Self esteem problems because He always remembered. He never, like us, suffered from the dis-ease of Spiritual Amnesia.

Because of our hand me down, second hand, and borrowed beliefs, some of us think this life, this drama which we have created for this moment, is a test. Depending on whether we pass or fail, we are going to die and either spend eternity burning in a place called hell or we are going to die to go spend eternity in a place called heaven. There we will receive a crown and we will walk streets of gold and sit at Jesus' feet learning all the things we don't know and continue to praise Him forever.

I believe NOW is the day of salvation, NOW is the day to learn, NOW is the day to praise God, for we are experiencing eternity NOW. There is no beginning or ending of eternity. There is no other future of which we are assured, there is only the NOW.

We view or have viewed this life on earth as a place where a loving compassionate merciful gracious judgmental God is up in the sky with a check list for each one of us, and when we die, just like Santa Clause, He will check it twice, to see if we were naughty or nice or if we believed in Him enough and did more good things than bad things, so He can see if we deserve to enter heaven and how many stars we get in or crown. Because we never really know for sure if we are going to make it, we live with the fear that we might make one to many mistakes and thus find ourselves in a burning hell where we will not only spend eternity burning, but having to smell the awful stench of other burning flesh. Even though some of us may believe that "once saved, always saved," if we ever really pondered on it and because some religions believe differently, we may have doubts whether that is true or not. There is always a little bit of fear that asks, "what if I'm wrong? What if I'm not doing things right enough or good enough to make it?"

Because of these fears that arise, (and of course we are told that it is the devil that causes them), we find it hard to trust, to really trust our health, our finances, or our life to someone who we have a relationship with only out of fear.

I'm wondering if this, also, is where we start to develop an ambivalence toward religion, spirituality, and God. Again, we may feel, "what's the use."

The World Book Encyclopedia describes the word ambivalence as a term used by psychiatrists to describe feelings that are equally strong, but directly opposed. For example, if one person has feelings toward another that includes both love and hate (fear) like or dislike, or friendliness and enmity, psychiatrists say that his feelings are ambivalent. Psychoanalysts have found that when one person's feelings toward another are strong, they are almost always ambivalent. Sometimes only one of the ambivalent feelings, such as love, is conscious. The other ambivalent feeling, hate (or fear) is wholly unconscious.

The unconscious is the same as the subconscious. It is a term used to describe mental processes such as thoughts, ideas, and feelings that go on in people's minds without their being aware of them. Though this theory was first studied in the 1800's by the French neurologist Jean Charcot and his students by means of hypnosis, it was Sigmund Freud who became aware of the importance of unconscious thoughts and feelings in the field of human psychology. With his method of psychoanalysis he was able to prove that unconscious thoughts and feelings not only produce the symptoms of many types of mental illness, but that they are also of basic importance in the way the minds of normal people work.

From our first day on the planet our subconscious has been fed. Our subconscious is like a refrigerator. Until we became an adult, everyone in our life puts into our refrigerator the same things that someone else had put in theirs. As an adult we can remove those things or thoughts that are no longer serving us for our good and replace them with healthy things or thoughts. If you are wondering what to replace those unhealthy thoughts with, Bro. Paul recommended something in Philippians 4:4-8.

Folks, our refrigerators aren't just filled with unhealthy things from our past. We allow it to be filled with unhealthy things daily by our choice of friends, work environment, relationships, entertainment, and even some of our religious teaching. Look at the music and the entertainment industry. We sing about being unfaithful and about our needy co-dependent life. We see it along with the violence that it invites, portrayed on television and in the movies. Maybe, because we can relate, we feel that our life is normal.

When our knowledge goes beyond this human life filled with whose cheating on who, addictions, abuse and other such issues, we no longer have the need to feed our soul or subconscious with those thoughts. I'm wondering how much, by feeding our minds with such negative thoughts, that we are perpetuating the challenges that come into our life.

It's perfectly okay to choose to do this because it is in experiencing the pain that we eventually wake up and start learning, remember? The entertainment industry gives us what they believe we want. If we buy it or go see it, they believe they need to make more of the same. Again what they are portraying is the way they as humans see life, and we go see it because that is the way we, as humans, see life.

I am pleased to see healthier movies and TV programs coming out and sneaking in a little thought about spirituality. I'm glad that we are being given more choices.

If we want to see violence and pain we don't have to watch a movie. All we have to do is turn on the news. After all this IS real life, real things happening to real people. A few years ago I asked myself what good did it do for me to watch the news. After the program was over I felt frustrated, angry, and helpless at what I had watched and knowing there was nothing I could do to help take away someone's pain or right a wrong. I would ask God to help the people find peace and good in their situations and with their challenges. Later, I felt that I could help people more by spending my time volunteering at a nursing home, taking care of children, taking the children to the park to pick up trash, or creating beautiful things such as this book, workshops, and retreats that might would be a vehicle to help such people find peace and good in life's challenges. I believe if there is something important that I need to know that's in the news, there will be a way made for me to hear.

I love history, maybe because of it being a part of me or me being a part of it, I don't know. In today's real history making stories, journalism sandwiches in the pain, suffering and all the hellaciousness of the universe. Once in a while like a rare gem or a breath of fresh air, we hear of some "Good" coming from it.

Some will have the idea that I'm like the ostrich with my head in the sand. Some will say that I have my head in the clouds.

Some may think I have a Pollyanna attitude, I have a Forest Gump mentality or that I'm out of touch with reality. That's okay because my ego had the same thoughts. At least I know who has control of my remote control.

The human self or ego feeds on the illusion of evil, the pain and suffering. It points a finger saying, "see, there is no good. All is ugly. There is no hope." And then we wonder why there are so many people depressed.

Why do we continue in the bondage of these lies? Why do we just accept these lies as the way things are while deep in our side our neglected soul cries out, "These are lies, don't listen, get up from the lethargic bed of ignorance where you have been far too long and search for, claim, receive the Truth that has been and will be yours for eternity. Please allow your Higher Self to take back the remote control of your life."

Folks, if the world is going to hell in a handbasket, who in the hell do you think is carrying the handbasket? Hello!!! What are we teaching the ones who will be carrying it the next generation?

Many of us wander through life in a sleepy unconscious state feeling we are just victims of life. It's time to wake up and make responsible choices through the guidance of the Holy Spirit.

For most of our lives we have invested our souls in this human existence which is not eternal. Because of fears of rejection and loss we have become, in an unhealthy way, attached to people, things, religions, beliefs, traditions, and everything that is not eternal. Thus when any of these seem jeopardized or it looks like we are going to lose something, our ego doesn't like that because it, too, is not eternal and fear sets in.

Many psychologists believe that infants are born without emotions. They believe that children learn emotions just as they learn to read and write. Psychologists also believe there are only two types of emotions; negative and positive.

A Course in Miracles also teaches there are only two emotions; fear and Love. I agree that fear is a learned emotion as is human love. When the ego decided to exercise its "free will," it tried to duplicate or counterfeit God's Divine Love, so the ego created human love. However, deep down it knew it wasn't going to work so then fear was created and the ego became like a frightened hungry wounded animal. We must remember that we came to this planet as Spiritual Beings, only with God's Divine Love so that we can be the expression and manifestation of God, who is Love.

Fear is an emotional response. The negative energy from fear triggers chemicals to be released into the bloodstream and physical changes occur in the body. You will notice some of these changes by increased heartbeat, harder more rapid breathing, flushed face, and tightness in the chest, just to remind you of a few. Sometime these emotions are so painful our body develops defense mechanisms such as denial, forgetting, numbing, and disassociation. These defense mechanisms are considered the cause of mental illnesses. It's my belief that mental illness is a manifestation of our neglecting our soul's cry for knowledge and for us to try to remember who we are, where we came from, why we are here, and where we are going. It is a cry from our soul to be healed from our dis-ease called Spiritual Amnesia.

Only the positive energy of Love can heal our Spiritual Amnesia. Thus only Love can heal mental illness. Thus only Love can heal any dis-ease. Thus only Love can heal the planet. As Marianne Williamson says, "We must return to Love."

Because we are Spiritual Beings we have to soar higher in our consciousness than our limited five sense humanness. We have to look beyond what we experience with our five senses. We have to believe, (this is salvation) and trust in the power within each of us. Again, it's the same power that dwells in all of us, it's just that some are more aware of it than others. There are not different levels of Spirituality, only different levels of awareness and remembrance.

The World Book Encyclopedia describes amnesia as the inability to recall or remember some or all past experiences. Persons who suffer from amnesia lose the ability to recall past experiences, but not the ability to memorize. They may even leave their homes, wander for a while, and start a new life somewhere else. This wandering while experiencing amnesia is called, fugue. Amnesia may be caused by either emotional shock or physical injury. In emotional shock, amnesia is usually restricted to experiences closely related to the cause of the shock. Doctors treat amnesia of emotional origin by hypnosis (meditation is a form of hypnosis) or with certain drugs. Physical injury, such as a heavy blow to the head, may cause actual changes in the brain, making recall impossible. According to The World Book Encyclopedia, memory is the ability to keep a mental record of earlier experiences. Basically, memory is learning. Psychologists use three methods to determine how much a person remembers. These methods are: (1)recall, which is to see how much we can remember, (2)recognition, which is to see if we recognize anything that might be triggered to make us remember, and (3)relearning, which is like starting all over.

Somewhere between our innocent infant self and adulthood, we developed Spiritual amnesia and forgot who we were, where we came from, what our purpose is and where we will be returning. However, it's okay because whether during this life time or another, we will remember. I guess this is predestination.

I'm still learning to be patient, to accept, and to Love as I remember what I've forgotten. I'm no longer as concerned with the whens, wheres, whys, and hows. I want to live today to the fullest. I want to get every good thing I can from life. At the same time, I want to give everything I can back to it. I am positively, undeniably, unmistakably happier than I have ever been in my life.

"Blessed be God, even the Father of our Lord Jesus Christ, the Father of mercies and the God of all comfort; Who comforts us in all our tribulation, that we may be able to comfort them which are in any trouble, by the comfort wherewith we ourselves are comforted of God." 2nd Corinthians 1:3-4

This is the ultimate purpose for this book. Because my Father comforted me, He provided loving understanding supporters, the wisdom from my therapists, great books, His continual validations, and His amazing other "God Deals" along the way, I have no choice but to share my story with total confidence and assurance that it will give you comfort where ever you are on this exciting adventure called life. I do this as a gift back to my Father and to you.

I am enlightened enough to know that everyone will not be receptive to my offering comfort, encouragement, inspiration, and Love. Jesus Christ's teachings on living under Grace instead of the law wasn't accepted by everyone. He was labeled as a rebel in his time. Yet, He lived what He taught. As I said before it's as though I'm trying to feed and comfort a hungry wounded animal, but because of its fears and ignorance, it chooses to attack and destroy instead of seeing and accepting the Good which our Higher Self offers. Because I know that my continuing is important for the continual healing of the Spiritual Amnesia that is limiting humanity today, I will continue the task that is before me.

I can see that the Mental Health Profession has the greatest opportunity, now more than ever, to be a part of this healing. In order for this to happen, I see that in some cases the verse that reads, "*Physician, heal thyself*" must be practiced first.

I believe there comes a time in everyone's life when our soul can be still no longer and we wake up, look around and ask the questions, "What am I doing here? What is happening to me? Who am I? How did I get here? Is this all there is to life? Where and how do I find happiness?

Spiritual Amnesia

At this very moment, as I write this, there is a miraculous healing taking place through out our Universe. More people than ever before are becoming aware of the need for this healing. Those in some recovery groups are receiving it. Those in some religious organizations are receiving it. Those in some psychotherapy sessions are receiving it. Those attending certain seminars, workshops, retreats, and Visions Quests are receiving it. Some who read every self-help book that they can get their hands on are receiving it.

Those of us who are consciously receiving our healing are willingly and joyfully joining together to become teachers and healers to share our observations with others. The more unified we become in this endeavor the faster the Universe will become aware that there is a need for such healing. As teachers and healers, we lovingly share the personal knowledge which we have found. We do this with the belief that it will ignite with a tiny spark within the soul of those who are ready to recognize and begin their healing journey. We do not give healing. We live our lives as reminders that healing is found within.

Amnesia is the complete or partial loss of memory due to injury to the brain which is caused by dis-ease or a shock. Humanity is suffering from Spiritual Amnesia and is now seeking for and receiving healing from this malady.

For most of us, our arrival to this planet was a traumatic experience as we made our way through the birth canal arriving into a less than gentle, cold, hurried, noisy, bright environment. This was quite the opposite from the gentle, warm, relaxed, quiet, dark place we left. In a matter of minutes we experienced our first shock. However, because of our unadulterated Spiritual wisdom, we quickly adjusted and adapted to our new environment.

For the first few months after we arrived here on this

planet, as the pure innocent precious miraculous perfect Spiritual Beings that we are, we remembered who we were, where we came from, and where we were going. Most of our mind was the Conscious awareness of our Higher Spiritual Self.

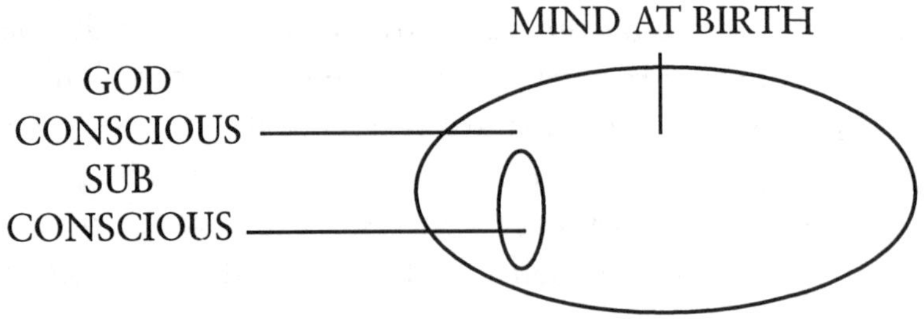

However, most of us went home from the hospital that day with a family who was suffering from Spiritual Amnesia and immediately they started programming our minds with their human knowledge, ideas, beliefs, and perceptions. Some of what they fed us was what had been handed down to them. As we got older our school teachers, our Sunday school teachers and everyone that came into our lives, programmed us with their knowledge, values, and beliefs.

One such belief was that there was some things we were to be afraid of. One of those was something known as "evil." We were to be constantly on guard, looking over our shoulders, and around the corner expecting "it" to jump out at us anytime. We weren't told what it would do to us, just that it was very powerful and we were to be deathly afraid of it. What this programming does, is to introduce us to one of our constant hindrances that keeps us from remembering who we are and what we came here to do. This emotion, which becomes one of our greatest teachers and tester of our faith, is known by the name of fear.

Later on we might have even been told that we should be afraid of the man in the sky. He made us and we were to spend the rest of our lives trying to be perfect and serve Him. If we didn't we would be punished by burning in a place called hell. Living in fear instead of faith takes the joy and peace out of our life.

Our story is similar to the story of when Adam and Eve experienced Spiritual Amnesia. After eating of the forbidden fruit from the tree, which contained the KNOWLEDGE of good and evil, they lost their innocence. This shock threw them into partial Spiritual Amnesia. They forgot that God was the only Power. It's because of this same knowledge of evil (we already knew about the Good), we lost our innocence. This was another traumatic experience which continued the dis-ease which would injure our mind and would eventually contribute to our own complete or partial Spiritual Amnesia.

As we grew in age, we experienced challenges and encountered circumstances that further programmed us to believe that there was another power as great as or greater than God the Good. By acknowledging another power, this takes away or diminishes, in our mind, God's Power or our Higher Self Power that dwells within us. Eventually our beautiful pure positive Spiritual consciousness is being over grown by the negative human ego consciousness, which is the complete opposite and a constant reminder of the first opposites we were introduced to upon our arrival here to the planet.

From then on, more than likely, we were constantly being fed a diet of negativity and fear. Just like we, who are health conscious know, there is a big difference in the health and in the performance of a body fed a diet that is high in fat and one that is fed a diet low in fat. It is the same with our mind. If it is fed an unhealthy diet it will become dis-eased. Thus more injury and more amnesia. We start experiencing self doubt, self blame, self judgment, self comparison, and self criticism. Because we are to love others as we love ourselves, we start transferring all this judgment, comparison, and criticism on to others. We start to react from fear instead of act with love to people and circumstances around us. Eventually, all this will bring us to a place where we will seek for healing.

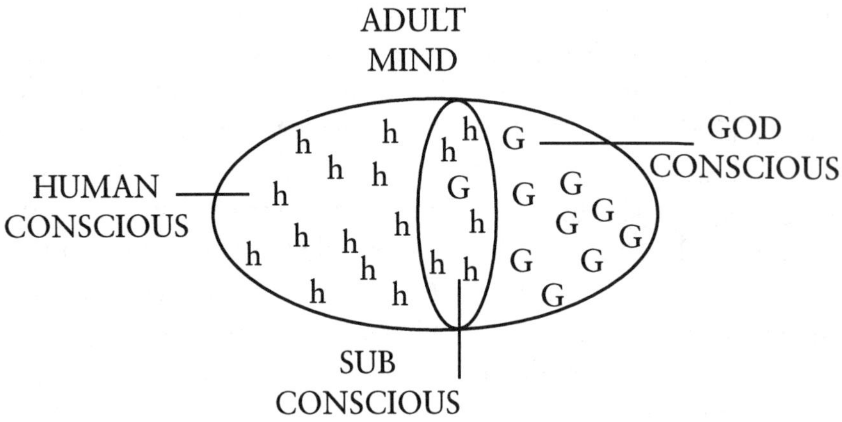

There will come a time in everyone's life when our soul starts having flashbacks of the knowledge of who we are, a perfect Spiritual Being. Of course this causes some discomfort within because some of it just doesn't compute. For years we have been programmed how bad and imperfect we were. We felt unlovable, unworthy, and invaluable. We may even find ourselves feeling helpless and hopeless thus we find ourselves in a depression.

Through grace our soul starts trying to tell us that there is something really important and wonderful that we need to be remembering, but, before we can get a grasp on it, we lose that thought or that feeling. This causes more pain and unrest. It feels like we lost something, but we don't know how to find it because we don't know what we are looking for. It feels so frustrating. We feel angry and we are not even sure at what. We become restless, dissatisfied, and discontented with our family, with our job, life, and ourselves. We feel trapped and want to run, but we don't know what we are running from or where we should be running to. It seems nothing goes right, everyone is out to make life hell for us. We feel we are on the perpetual merry-go-round and we want off, but we don't know how to stop it. We may even wonder sometime if we might be losing our mind. So we look for ways to cope with the pain as we live with the fear. We are ignorant of the fact that these are wake up calls so that we can begin our healing. This is God's Grace going before us.

While trying to numb or deaden the pain and discomfort, we may unconsciously look towards unhealthy relationships. We are trying to find someone to make us feel loved and happy. Someone who will kiss our boo boo to soothe our pain and make it go away. We go from one relationship to another without success. We may become addicted to alcohol, drugs, gambling, sex, work, television or anything that might give us a few minutes of what looks like pleasure and take our minds off the discomfort. For some, the television remote control is the only thing in life they feel they have control of.

Some may even try the psychedelic drugs from the sixties. I hear that there may be a revival of some of these same drugs because they are being researched to see about prescribing them in safe doses, of course, to numb the discomfort. I've also heard that prozac is being prescribed for children. I see this as only a false or temporary "fix" like a band aid. It will not cure the Spiritual Amnesia, which is the real problem. The people I see benefiting the most from this are the doctors and developers of the drugs. The patient, as long as he is sedated, will have a harder chance to be healed, therefore will have to keep coming back, but this is called legal drug trafficking.

I have the faith that one day those in the mental health field will awaken from their own Spiritual Amnesia and remember what psychology really is, "the study of the soul." Right now instead of studying or caring for the soul, the studying goes into developing drugs to help balance the chemicals in the brain. Forget about searching for the internal cause or offering a spiritual approach, just give them a prescription.

I can understand the tendency to stay away from the subject of religion because of the spiritual abuse that has taken place with so many. Religion is the last thing we want to hear about. This is where personal searching for Truth is so important. We aren't talking about religion. We are talking about our personal relationship with the God of our understanding.

It is usually the unhealthy relationships, depression, mood disorders, and addictions that move us along on our journey to the teachers and healers who are waiting to remind us of the knowledge of The GOOD within ourselves. This will ignite the tiny spark in our souls to search. This will lead us on a journey of healing and discovery as we get back in touch with our Higher Self. It's our Higher Self, that spiritual part of us, that will help us regain our memory and recover from our Spiritual Amnesia. It is then we will remember the power we have within us as our healing takes place.

The miraculous thing about our awesome mind is that all dis-ease can be reversed. When we choose to answer our "Wake Up Call" and we begin our healing journey, we have to start by looking at our soul wounds which were caused by the events and experiences from our past. We must grieve and grieve and grieve some more. A part of our healing is when we come to the realization that we were and are powerless over what happened to us back there; we can't change any of it, however, we do have power and control over the effects of it that we see manifested in our lives today. We will learn to release, let go, and deprogram the old negativity, beliefs, and knowledge that we learned while growing up that no longer serves any purpose in our life. Removing those things leaves a void that must be filled with consciously, willingly, and daily inputting the positive, the affirmative, and the good back into our minds. By bringing back or reprogramming these attributes, we will begin to remember what we all ready know, but have just forgotten.

Personally, I have found in my own healing experience

that it was necessary and accelerated my healing process when I practice and give as a gift back to the Universe the loving and compassionate art of forgiveness for myself and others. This is a powerful experience and a beautiful gift to give ourselves.

I can boldly offer my personal observation and share my experience because I've been there and am doing that. Because of regaining some of my memory, I can offer my personal observation with the belief that it will ignite that tiny spark in someone's soul...

It's Never Too Late To Learn

While playing in the back yard with the children on a sunny October morning, I heard squeals from my granddaughter Jessica and her friend Cade. They had found this exquisite creature that looked like a beautiful butterfly except that it's body was a lot larger. It was big and had magnificent grays and pinks on its body and wings. When it flew to the tree across the street, it soared like a bird instead of fluttering its wings gracefully like a butterfly. We looked in the encyclopedia, but didn't find it in the butterfly section. My wise daughter, Donna, suggested looking under moths. The only moth I had ever known was the kind that damaged our clothes. Imagine my surprise and delight when at the age of fifty two years and ten months, I was blest to have seen my first Pink-Spotted Hawk Moth. Guess we are never to old to learn something new if we just choose to accept the opportunity when it is presented to us.

Our Contribution

There will come a time in our recovery that we will have to answer the question: What do we gain or get from our continuing to carry around our old bag of stinky manure from the past?

I know it took a long time for us to be able to admit that we had this big smelly bag with us. We felt so ashamed and guilty for smelling the way we did. We tried to hide or disguise it because we thought we were the only person with such a bag. We tried to make it look and smell pretty.

Finally we found a safe place with a safe person to let it be seen. We gagged as we started to look at it, but she never gagged or at least she never let us see her gag. We found others that had bags of manure, too. We made a pack with them saying, "I will love and accept you even with your manure if you will love and accept me with mine."

After a while we accepted the fact that we did accumulated a lot of manure from our childhood. No one could deny that. We learned to put the blame on our perpetrators which was rightly so. We allowed ourselves to feel the feelings of anger, of betrayal, and all the other pain. This was necessary and it was a good thing. We spent a sufficient amount of time examining it, smelling it, getting it on ourselves and others. We may have buckled under the load a few times, but we managed to get up and continue on. We allowed it to slow us down, to hinder us from being free. We began to blame the bag for our not being able to follow our dreams. We spent so much energy carrying it that we had little energy for anything else. We may have even laid it down for a moment, but for some reason, we picked it back up.

It has been a long time now and we have become accustom to the weight and the smell. It doesn't seem to bother us that our friends don't call as often. We tell ourselves if they can't love me with my bag of manure then they aren't the kind of friends I need anyway.

I'm still wondering what good do we derive from occasionally opening the bag and taking a whiff? Do we want to make certain it is still there and it smells the same? Do we want to admire the color or the texture? Do we want to spread some on us hoping others will notice? Do we think smelling like manure will attract others to us? Most people don't care for the smell so they will stay away from us. I would imagine that the only people who we will attract will be people who can't smell our manure because their manure smells just as strong.

I wonder what would happen if all of us with our bags of manure, found a little piece of earth; we tilled it and we planted some flower seeds (forgiveness); all different kinds and colors representing all our differences. What then if we took our heavy bag of manure and lovingly scooped it out and spread it on the earth over those tiny seeds. Before long we would be gathering together to appreciate the beauty of the flowers. It wouldn't be long before we would have forgotten the heavy smelly bag of manure. We would just be in awe at the beauty of all the different flowers which we see blooming all over the earth. Though they were individually planted, it looks like one giant flower garden.

We would find that we were lighter on our feet and able to do a lot more. We would have nothing to blame for our not taking responsibility for our lives. We would develop new relationships with the other souls who came to enjoy the beauty of the flowers, also. We would find harmony and peace. We would experience joy and love. We would feel good within because we now contributed to the beauty of the earth instead of the stench of it.

I found that meditation and guided visualization were a big help in getting still and quiet. I've included a guided visualization titled "Surrender." If after reading it, you feel that it would be helpful, I invite you to record it in your own voice speaking slowly and quietly.

Surrender

A guided visualization

To help us get centered and more receptive, I invite you to empty your hands and set aside anything in your lap as well as in your mind that might hinder you from feeling totally and completely relaxed. Breathe in deeply and hold...., release slowly. Breathe in again and hold...., release. Breathe in once more and hold...., release. As you are becoming aware of the rhythm of your breathing and when you feel safe, I invite you to close your eyes. Stay aware of your breathing and as you breathe in, see yourself as breathing in calmness and peace. As you breathe out see yourself as allowing the stress, the hurries, and the business of the day to be released and leave your body. Again, as you breathe in allow yourself to breath in peace and calmness. Breathe out anything that would prevent you from accepting the peace and the calmness.

As you have become aware of your breathing, I, also, invite you to become aware of your feelings. Whatever you feel is perfectly all right. I give you permission to give yourself permission to feel. I give you permission to give yourself permission to express those feelings in a safe loving way. Be gentle, kind, and loving with yourself. This is your journey. This is your path. This is your time to heal. Your feelings are perfectly all right.

In our mind, as we walk along our path, we come to a beautiful natural stone bridge. It's a natural stone bridge because God put it there, Himself. On the side of the bridge we see large white stones and on those stones we see the word KNOWLEDGE etched in green as if the beautiful moss was somehow growing there. Crossing this bridge takes us from the "life's a bitch and then you die" attitude to "Life's a miraculous adventure" attitude. Crossing this bridge is our personal choice.

Before we step onto the bridge, somehow we know that we are about to have a beautiful experience. Instinctively, we know that where we are going, we will have no need for the old tapes we've heard all of our life, nor do we need our bag of manure, so we willingly, freely, consciously choose to leave them all on the path, knowing they will be there waiting for us if we choose to return.

As we take a deep breath and step onto the bridge, it's as if we have been taken by the hand and are now being led by angels. We have no fear for we know this is a Good thing. As we are led across the bridge, we hear the sound of the little brook below and when we look down we see beautiful green moss carpeted rocks. We stop for a moment just to enjoy the beauty and the quietness. Except for a few song birds, all we hear is the cool water gently flowing over the moss carpeted rocks and the sound of our own rhythmic breathing.

We leave the bridge and find ourselves at the entrance to a beautiful green lush forest. The trees appear tall and strong like mighty towers because of the huge trunks. There is a sense of protection and shelter and it feels so inviting. There are feelings of peace, serenity, healing, and rest as we step into this, natures' sanctuary.

Continuing along the path, it seems as if we are being led and we are the only one there. The brook seems to be following us, also. We may notice that the path, because it is going up the side of a mountain, has an incline in places and there may be roots and rocks along the way, but we don't feel the difference and we don't stumble because it's as if our feet are no longer touching the ground.

We see all kinds of colorful wildflowers growing. In one spot, nestled all by itself among the huge trunks of the tall trees, is a little bush with lacy green leaves and an abundance of delicate pink blossoms bursting forth with an intoxicating fragrance. Without saying a word out loud, but in our minds we hear the angels tell us that it is perfectly okay to stand out or to stand alone in our own individual beauty along with the other kinds of beauty in the universe. We don't have to be like or think like everything or everyone else around us. It's perfectly okay to be different, to look different and to smell different.

It is at this time we are brought into a space like no other. There is an opening through the tops of the trees that the sunlight is shining through. We stand in awe, in the stillness of this beautiful place. The rays of light stream in as if a spotlight straight from God is shining on this area. It is so bright that we can not, with our human eyes, look up into it. Even standing away from it, a certain flow of energy can be felt. It's the kind of energy that draws another into it. It's called Love. Something inside of us is quickened and we know this is where we are supposed to be and we know what we came here to do. We also know after we step into this Light that we will not step out as the same person we were when we stepped in. We also know this is a choice. We can turn around and leave right now and go back to our old path with our old familiar baggage, our complacent disorders and illnesses. Everything is waiting for us right where we left it on the other side of the bridge. If we want to turn back, now is the time to do it.

For you who, in your mind, chose to journey on with us, welcome to the beginning of your new miraculous life. By stepping into the Light you will have made the choice to change the course of your life, forever. By stepping into the Light you are symbolically saying to God, "I have not done such a great job on my own with my life. Thank you for the pain and the mistakes you have allowed me to experience for they have brought me to this moment; this moment when I remember who I am in You; this moment when I, with thanksgiving, willingly, consciously, and lovingly surrender and give control of my life back to you as a love gift. I ask not only that you guide me, but that you live, move, and have your being in and through me. I thank you for the opportunity to be your representative here on this planet. I let go and release any and all things that would hinder or interfere in my mission for being here to share how I found peace within my Self, by being the expression of God just by loving. I let go and release any and all things that would hinder or interfere with my receiving all the abundance, all the prosperity, all the perfect emotional, mental, and physical health, and all the other Good that you so delight in giving to me for your good pleasure. I know these gifts are already mine because I am your child. I, with thanksgiving claim them and receive them in the lovely name of my elder brother, Jesus Christ. So be it and so it is."

As we step into this Light, we can still hear the sound of the brook. We can still hear the sounds of the birds. As we step into this Light, this spotlight from God, something mysteriously, miraculously wonderful happens in us. We feel as if we are bathed in this Light. It feels as if warm healing oil is being poured over and through us as it enters in through the top of our head and it goes through our brain, passing on down through the back of our head, the front of our head, the sides of our head, opening our ears to hear, opening our eyes to see, opening our nose to smell. It's passing inside our mouth permeating our tongue, to taste and see that this is good. The Light continues to bath and heal as it goes through our neck, taking with it any feelings of stress or tension. It pours over our shoulders, through our arms, down through to our hands where we are taught to touch. At the same time, it is going through our shoulders continuing down our back, the upper part of our back, the middle of our back, the lower part of our back, over our buttocks, down through our sides. It is going through the front of us, our chest, all of our internal organs are being bathed with this Light. Everything is being put where it should be in its perfect place. All of our bones are in the right place, all of our organs are in the right place, all of our life blood is flowing and circulating at the perfect rhythm the way it's supposed to, creating perfection and harmony in our body. Our joints are being freed from any aches and pains of arthritis or old injuries. All of our organs are now working perfectly. The healing Light continues down our body, down through our thighs, our legs. We have such strength in our legs. Through our knees, through the lower part of our legs, our calves, our ankles. Ankles that were once weak are now becoming stronger. It flows down to our feet all the way out of our toes, back into Mother Earth.

Let's stand here a moment in this healing Light as it continues, without stopping bathing our body in its warmth. All the energy is coming straight from the sun, straight from God. From the top of our head, all the way down, through our feet, back into Mother Earth, where it goes back to God. Just stand and breath it in. In the back ground we can still hear the brook and the birds singing. We can hear all these things as we feel a gentle breeze on our cheeks as if angels wings are touching us as they are fluttering by. We are enveloped in this Light. We are surrounded in this Light. We are protected in this Light. Nothing, nothing at all can harm us. There is only Good in this Light, there is only Love in this Light. As we feel this energy going through our bodies perfecting anything that we feel is imperfect, we can feel this energy perfecting all the parts of our bodies radiating through our bodies and it stays there. It doesn't leave. It leaves the energy there. It leaves the Love there. Breathe it in. We can't look up at it because it is just to bright, but we can close our eyes and feel the warmth. The warmth is from God's Love. The warmth is the healing energy, the healing oil passing through and healing any past wounds any soul wounds, anything, any aches whether they are emotional, or physical. They are being healed as this Light touches each cell in our body.

We are conscious and know that once we step out from this Light, we will never again be the same. We will leave this space a different person than we were when we entered. This space will always be here for us to return to as often as we need it. This is a place of Love, it is a refuge, it's a healing place for body, soul, and spirit. We can hear the birds in the back ground. It's a beautiful place. God is here. This is God because all of this is God. When we leave this place, because we know that we are a different person, we are filled with more Love, we have been healed. We know we are to take responsibility for our lives. We are to take responsibility for our choices. Never more will we be unconscious, never more will we be asleep to our choices, never more will we be ignorant to our choices. We will know that God, through this Light, is giving us wisdom and is giving us knowledge. He will from now on remind us of our choice. Whatever choice we make will be the right choice for that moment. Sometimes the choice may cause us pain and that is okay, for we will learn from it. Sometime the choice is there to teach us, and to help us grow. As we leave, we choose to venture out and take a different path. We choose to carry with us this Light for it is a part of us now. As we go, we know that if we share this Light, it will continue to grow within us and will shine through us to those who are unaware of their own Light. By seeing ours, they will remember theirs. Pretty soon the planet will be illuminated with everyone's Light. This is our purpose, for we are Spiritual Beings temporally housed in the form of a human. We are in this world, but are not of it. We are no longer limited to our humanness. And so it is. Thank you Mother/ Father God.

Have I Found My Self?

In my search for my Self, have I found me? After the first year and a half of excellent therapy, support groups, lots of reading, writing, grieving and changing, I had found bits and pieces of myself. Like a puzzle, I painstakingly and patiently tried fitting them together. One of the problems I found was that it was like a two sided puzzle. One side was the false, or as Yvonne Kaye calls it, the impostor self that I had lived all those years. The other side was my real Self that had been buried all those years. It was at that time that I was privileged to see into the future and I saw what my new Self looked like and that helped in putting the pieces together.

One of the challenges that I found was that some of my false self pieces looked a lot like my real Self. The only way I could tell the differences was when the piece just didn't quite fit into the new picture.

As I picked up some of the pieces, I found that they were completely reversible and would fit in either picture; My sense of humor, my spontaneity, my love for God and His beauty that surrounds me, my being everyone's mother, and my love for children are just a few that comes to mind. At that time I guess the answer was YES and NO. Yes, in that I could see what I was going to look like and No in that I didn't have it completely together yet.

One thing I have learned is that this Recovery journey is like any other trip. It's important to enjoy the time spent traveling to the destination. It's the adventures, the investigating, the learning experiences, and yes, even the stopping along the way that is the real journey, not the destination itself. That's a whole different adventure in it's self.

So, today, almost five years into the journey and after the research, I can say *Yes, I have found my Self.* As I sat here going over the words in this book the night before I take it to be printed, I know that I have found my real Self between the covers of this book. For between these covers, deep within the core of each word is a celebration of Grace, Faith, Courage, Healing, Wisdom, Love, Peace, Joy, Life, and other such Miracles. Inside these covers which signify there is a celebration, I find an expression and manifestation of God. I'm wondering if maybe that's why I chose to not have my picture on the cover. I don't want to be thought of in this physical form. That's not the real me. Yes, I know without a doubt who I am. I hope by my sharing with you of my personal theory, you are clear that I am clear. To those who only understand with the human mind, what I found won't make sense. Right about now they are shaking heads in disbelief. It's perfectly okay.

What I'm sharing did not come from books or seminars, although later I did receive validation from them. Knowledge that is received from someone else is not wisdom. It's information about something that the person who is sharing has learned for themselves. It's second hand or borrowed. What I share came from my search within myself and was revealed by God through His marvelous Grace. It did not come easy and some of the information was just as shocking to me, in my humanness, as it might be to you. However, this is Truth that I know. I share this with the hope that you will be motivated to do your own inner search for Truth.

Knowing something or someone is quite different than knowing about something or someone. There is a subject which only a certain group knows well. No other person anywhere can ever really know this subject like we do. There are shelves and shelves of books on the subject; there are videos; there are stories of other people's experiences; and there are workshops; all filled with important facts and material to help anyone learn about this subject. All this wealth of information is so vital because it helps dispel some of the fear. However, until someone experiences for themselves the morning sickness, the swollen ankles, the hot flashes, endures the doctor visits, the mood swings, the backaches; until one experiences the first flutter of life growing inside of them, the peacefulness, the glow that comes from the knowledge of the miracle growing within them; until one experiences the incredible love that grows for this little person to whom there has been no formal introductions; until one experiences that tinge of fear when you realize that labor has begun; when you experience the doubt and wonder, as if it mattered now, if you are really ready for this change in your lifestyle, or what if you don't know everything you need to know? Until you experience holding that beautiful warm little miracle that just spent nine months safe and warm inside of you; that you willingly with love shared your body with; until you hold that precious little miracle to your breast for the first time and you feel that bond between you that absolutely no one else will ever be able to share; only then will you really know the joy of giving birth. Until you actually have the experience, you only know about it.

The miracle that I have experienced in my search or my research and the Truth that I have found is no less miraculous than giving birth.

In Closing

I feel so privileged, and blest to have been able to share this small part of my celebration of my life with you. You have the choice to take what you want and leave the rest. I trust that you received what you needed for your own personal journey. I hope this book is one that you can pick up and read over and over again when you need a reminder of what an awesome God we have in charge and what a miracle of creation you are in your own uniqueness. You are one of a kind. You are wonderfully and beautifully made. You are unconditionally loved and accepted just as you are.

I have so much more to share, but it isn't the time. As you are reading this book, I will be finishing the next one, *I've Crossed Over the Bridge.*

I'm so excited for you as you make your journey. I'm excited for you as you experience your own miracles. It doesn't matter whether you are nineteen or ninety nine, it's never to late to start remembering. We are blest with a fresh new day every twenty four hours.

It's not easy closing this letter to you, but I would like to leave with you some things to keep in mind;

(1.) Just like our life's journey is personal, so is our relationship with our Higher Power as we understand Him or Her. It is our responsibility to do our part to develop and make that relationship grow into as strong, close, and intimate one as we want. It is our choice. We have the "free will."

(2.) Get Knowledge. We are all given the gift of curiosity and a built in desire to search for the hidden Truth or hidden things of God. Honoring this longing is caring for the soul and makes it healthy. Not honoring it makes us physically sick in our bodies, and mentally and emotionally sick in our souls.

(3.) Take the knowledge and make it your wisdom by internalizing it and using it. Only then will you know that you know that you know.

(4.) Be aware of the miracles around you. Purposefully and consciously look for them. Make this a daily habit.

(5.) Recognize that you are a precious miracle, an unique creation of God. At the same time remember like the fingers are connected to our hand, so are all of we, the whole Universe, connected to the same Power of the Universe.

(6.) When we ask Spirit for Wisdom, the soul manifests, through Grace, what we need for that lesson. The pain, whether it is caused by ourselves or someone else, and the mistakes we make are our teachers. These lessons are for our spiritual growth. Always look for the Good in all situations. Remembering and practicing this simple Truth makes life a lot more peaceful.

(7.) Purpose. Find and remember your real purpose for being on this planet. It's not to be a doctor, lawyer, mom, teacher or any of the other jobs out there. They, like our relationships, are only here to provide us with the experiences to practice our real purpose for being here, which is to be an expression and manifestation of Love or God.

I want to share with you two things that my first wise therapist shared with me. One is; *the sun is always shinning, even behind the clouds.* Even if our life seems full of clouds or our thinking seems cloudy, we always have the Light within and we can go there for wisdom and guidance. The other bit of wisdom is; *the Chinese have two characters for the word CRISIS. One means danger and one means* ***opportunity.*** When we are faced with what seems to be difficult challenges; when we have lost all hope and we feel helpless; when we feel completely out of control of our life; we can choose to give up to the point of addictions, disease, or even suicide or we can see it as an opportunity to look to the Power within and ask for wisdom and guidance. It's up to us to choose which way we want to accept the crisis or challenges that come into our life. They are given to us as turning points or wake up calls. They are given to us as part of a stage of our transformation.

Because this letter is written with the hope of provoking thoughts and feelings, I welcome the opportunity to hear of your celebration of the miracles you encounter as you journey here in a world that is not your home.

If you want to write and reserve your personal limited numbered copy of our next book, *I've Crossed Over the Bridge,* please do so. In it I will share what I've learned about subjects such as:

Knowledge and Wisdom, Ignorance and Fear, Choices and Responsibilities, Body/Soul/Spirit, Change Brings Recovery/Recovery Brings Changes, Our Journey is Personal, Losses/Grief/

Depression, Therapy/Therapist, Thoughts/Feelings of Suicide, Higher Power/God of our Understanding, The Abuse of our Spirituality, Forgiveness, Importance of Faith/Hope/Trust/Belief, Importance of Prayer/Meditation/Journaling, Death/A Celebration of Life.

I am also looking into creating poetry on tape using selected poems to create certain themes such as, *A Celebration* and *I'm Drunk on Life* and *Don't Ever Wanna Be Sober, Again.*

As I end this, I feel like I'm ending a letter to a dear friend. I wish I could meet each of you personally and hear your story. I wish for you sunshine after rain and joy after pain. Remember, we're one day closer to the next time I write you and we're one day closer to the healing of the dis-ease, Spiritual Amnesia. I wish for you all a healthy happy life as you continue on with your own adventures ahead. God Bless each of you and may you continue to grow IN HIM as you remember.

Celebrating in Him,

Lorraine Brown
P.O. Box 871381
Mesquite, Texas 75187

P.S. All I have to do is look at my remarkable incredible creative life which has been hidden all this time, of which I wasn't aware until I chose to go searching for it and now I unmistakably know:

YES, I BELIEVE IN AND CELEBRATE MIRACLES !!!!!!

Mini Workbook or Journal

This is for your personal use to make this book personally yours.

Date: ________ Time: ________

Some of my questions are:

Date: ________ Time: ________

If I could ask God three questions they would be:

Date: ________ Time: ________

My personal theory about life is:

Date: _________ Time: _________

My feelings about what I've read are:

A Gift For You

30% Off

to be applied toward tuition for any

Celebration of Miracles

Retreat or Workshop

Signature: ______________________________

- -

YES! Please contact me with information about:

[ ] Quantity discounts on *In Search of My Self, A Celebration of Miracles*
[ ] Weekend Miracle Awareness Retreat and Celebration
[ ] *A Celebration of Miracles* Workshop
[ ] Having Lorraine Brown speak at my convention
[ ] Having Lorraine Brown speak at my high school
[ ] Having Lorraine Brown speak with my recovery group*
[ ] Having Lorraine Brown speak with my church group*

Name ____
Address ____
City ____________________ State __________ Zip ____________
Home Phone ______________ Work Phone _________________

Please enclose a Stamped, Self-Addressed # 10 Envelope for rapid reply.

*Love Offering

Acceptable as payment along with deposit
as registration for any

Celebration of Miracles

Workshop or Retreat.

To redeem this gift certificate,
send with your registration fee.

Mail To:

Miracle Creations

P.O. Box 871381

Mesquite, Texas 75187